THE USE
OF COLOR
IN INTERIORS

THE USE
OF COLOR
IN INTERIORS

Albert O. Halse

New York
San Francisco
McGRAW-HILL BOOK COMPANY
Toronto
London
Sydney

THE USE OF COLOR IN INTERIORS

ISBN 07-025618-7

34567890 HDBP 754321

FOREWORD

COLOR is a very important part of our lives. We are surrounded by it; we select our clothes, automobiles, houses, paintings, and even food packages by it. It is used to make us happy, to make us hungry, to promote serenity, and to encourage piety. It invites us into one architectural space and drives us out of another.

A number of excellent books have been written on the history, chemistry, and psychology of color. Much has been written about color for merchandising. Individual books on furniture, fabrics, carpets, and the decorative arts are readily available; one may easily observe the manner in which the great architects and interior designers have used the information found in them. Numerous color-notation systems are available. One may, if he wishes, examine the color lines of various materials that are available for use in interior work. Several "how-to-do-it" books which discuss color have been written. Almost daily, question-and-answer columns on the use of color are printed in newspapers, and the subject is discussed on radio and television.

This book, however, is analytical in nature. It has been written to provide the reader with the reasons behind the selections of color and combinations thereof. Each selection must include proper consideration of all contributing factors. A short history of the use of color is presented so that the reader will understand present-day uses of color in terms of the past and recognize that he must be part of the change that occurs around him. Technological and sociological background is provided for the same reason.

A discussion of the various color systems and their use provides information which is elsewhere hard to find and difficult to understand. Here the author has analyzed and compared the various systems so that they can be easily understood and used. With the background provided here, the reader can experiment with any color system as deeply as he wishes. The reader is also introduced to useful up-to-date technical information, such as the relationship between color and artificial light, as well as information about the psychological aspects of the uses of color. The author introduces the reader to the colors of furniture, furnishings, and built-in materials. In short, the reader is given the opportunity to look behind the scenes so that he can understand the factors governing the professional selection of color schemes. Given the principles described herein, the architect or the interior designer can solve any color problem.

Architectural design changes, and color in architecture changes with it. Furthermore, each color problem is unique; its successful solution depends, therefore, on a proper understanding of the particular problems involved. An understanding of the underlying principles for the use of color given in this book will enable the reader to adapt to new situations as they arise.

Albert O. Halse

CONTENTS

chapter one

FACTORS CONTRIBUTING TO CONTEMPORARY COLOR USAGE

T H I S book is devoted to a study of the contemporary use of color in the fields of architecture and interior design. We shall take a fleeting look at the historical use of color, since this will help us understand why we use color as we do today. We can thoroughly appreciate the use of color in other periods only if we know the general history of those periods. Many books are available for this purpose. We should look at the manner in which the scientist and painter look at color, but we must never confuse these approaches with the arts of architecture and interior design: they are simply not the same. The skills and knowledge of the painter and other artists do not alone make them capable of using color in architecture or interior design any more than they make them architects; nor does the cold analysis of the scientist make him an expert in interior design. Each contributes and inspires, but the architect or interior designer alone devotes his lifetime to the application of color in genuine architectural situations.

People in all periods of history have contributed some knowledge to the use of color in architecture and interior design, and there have been rich periods and barren periods, periods during which a great deal of color was used and periods during which little color was used. Although it is not our intention to explore at length this history, a brief look at the most important historical periods is important to the understanding of today's use of color in architecture and interior design.

Prehistoric

In prehistoric times, the struggle for survival probably took all man's time and energy, but even when he killed or was himself in danger of being killed, the desire or need to express himself by drawing and by painting was strong enough to cause him to record in the feeble light of his caves those animals and objects that he saw during his daily existence. Some paintings may also have been made in his less permanent structures, but this we do not know. Using red and yellow ochre for drawing, and the same earth colors ground into a powder and mixed with animal fat for painting, ancient man produced pictures of bison, reindeer, wild boars, mammoths, and other animals, such as those on the walls of the cave at Altamira in Spain (15,000 B.C.) and at Font-de-Gaume in France (15,000 B.C.).

No one knows, of course, whether or not these drawings were for the purpose of guarding ancient man against evil or guaranteeing good hunting, but the author likes to feel that they were an attempt by man to brighten up a primitive living space and to make it something special and precious that he could retire to after the rigors of his almost impossible existence.

By the Mesolithic and Neolithic periods (20,000 to 2000 B.C.) men began to domesticate animals, to grow grain, and to live in permanent homes. Writing, indicated in the painted pebbles of the Azilians, began about 10,000 B.C. A few pieces of textiles, together with bundles of fibers, loom weights, and spinning whorls, have survived from this period.

Egypt

The materials at hand, the climate, and the richness of a civilization have always guided its craftsmen. In the realm of the pharaohs the sun was brilliant and the climate warm. Natural products such as timber, stone, and clay were available. Among the stones found most useful by the Egyptians were limestone, sandstone, syenite, and red granite.

In the Valley Temple of Kahfre (2850 B.C.) the supports and lintels were of red granite, well-proportioned, and cut and polished with proficiency. The floor was finished with slabs of alabaster. Columns in many other stone temples were richly decorated in color, and both exterior and interior walls were carved and painted. The ceilings of some temples were blue, probably to represent the sky, and the floors were often green, like the surrounding fields. Some authorities believe that color and decoration in ancient Egypt may have been symbolic; e.g., Osiris was usually represented by green, his wife Isis by blue, and their son Horus by white.

The paint, a kind of tempera, was apparently applied in flat tones with no blending or shading. While we can only surmise the many colors that were available to the Egyptian artist, we can see in the Metropolitan Museum of Art in New York City a fifteenth-century B.C. palette which contains medium and yellow ochre, terra-cotta red, turquoise blue, green, white, and black. These paints were no doubt made from burnt bones for black; malachite for green; oxide of iron for pink and red; red and yellow ochre; cobalt for blue; crystalline compounds of calcium, silica, and copper; and arsenic trisulfide, which made a bright lemon yellow.

Most murals were planned as story-telling devices which recorded daily life and religious functions. A frieze painted on plaster in the Tomb of Atet at Meidum

(2725 B.C.) has two handsomely drawn geese painted in black, gray, white, and red on a grayed background. The realistic foliage is rendered in a yellowish green. A painted limestone relief dated at 2550 B.C. includes golden yellow, black, gray, and orange. Later paintings included golden yellow, black, an orange red, and brilliant, yellowish green.

A painted limestone relief from Abydos (1991–1785 B.C.) shows the first use of cobalt blue with red figures in a geometric pattern. Cobalt blue, red, golden yellow, and black were used in a wall painting depicting birds being hunted with a throw stick (1400 B.C.).

Sculpture in the round included bowls, vases, heads of birds, and male and female figures. Many of these were finely painted. The sculptor of a statue of a princess (2900–2750 B.C.) used rock crystal for eyes, yellow for the skin, red for the lips, black for the hair and eyebrows, and red and blue for the necklace. A small figure of painted clay (237 B.C.) shows a painted green "skirt," and a clay vessel has a reddish-brown painted design.

Examples of wood furniture, used by royalty and the well-to-do, have been found, including chairs, chests, beds, and tables. Many are carved and painted, and such motifs as palm, lotus, papyrus, lion, cobra, and ibex were used as decoration. Although little is known of the colors used for Egyptian furniture, ivory and ebony were used as inlay, and gold ornament was applied to woodwork. The back support of the king's throne from the Tomb of King Tutankhamen and His Queen uses gilded wood with inlay of silver, faïence, and colored blue and green enamel (1340 B.C.). During the same period, dark blue was sometimes used against a lighter blue background.

The colors used in Ancient Egypt varied greatly from those of the prehistoric era (fifth to third millennia B.C.) and from those of the Ptolemaic and Roman periods (approximately 304–30 B.C.). In the Old Kingdom, painting was applied on reliefs; in the Middle Kingdom, the painters sometimes eliminated reliefs and painted directly on the walls or on stucco or plaster applied to rough walls. These wall paintings, a part of the Egyptian funerary art, were similar to those of the ancient periods. The later periods, dominated by aliens, show the use of traditional black, red, and white on light backgrounds, iridescent blue-purple-green faïence vessels, and bronze statues. Gradually, however, Greek and Roman elements appear in more definite form until even the god Horus is shown dressed as a Roman legionary.

The cultures of Egypt, Babylon, and Crete existed simultaneously for thousands of years. A similarity in the arts of these peoples indicates some interchange of ideas. The Babylonians used baked brick, glazed tiles, and friezes. On the island of Crete, the Palace of Knossos (3000–1500 B.C.) had foundations of stone blocks, and columns of wood with block bases, all brightly painted. There were wall frescoes depicting Cretan life, and there were colored plaster ceilings. Mural paintings included scenes of bullfights and ceremonies, and many scenes included pictures of fish, flowers, birds, and animals.

Greece

The Greeks, a colonizing and trading people who had contacts with the peoples of Egypt, Phoenicia, Babylonia, and Assyria, were inspired by the use of color in those lands. The climate of Greece, more diversified than that of Egypt, was semitropical, and there were variations in temperature and in the amount of moisture. The land was beautiful and inspirational. The homes of the early Greeks seem to have been unpretentious, and it could almost be said that they were more interested in life than they were in their physical surroundings. Religion played an important part in the life of the Greek, and he carved statues of his gods and built temples to protect these statues. During the early periods, the temples were of wood, but by 600 B.C. temples of stone began to appear. The proportions and details of these stone temples became more and more refined. The highest development of Grecian art occurred in the construction of a group of religious buildings, among them the Parthenon, on a hill called the Acropolis (447 B.C.). Marble, which took a high polish, soft white stone, and limestone were used for exteriors and interiors of these temples. All features of Greek architecture were functional. Structural surfaces were adorned only when such adornment emphasized, rather than hid, the structure. Color was used to accent the unity of design. Stone buildings such as those on the Acropolis were usually painted, the color being concentrated in the upper portions of the buildings. Blue and red were used in greatest amounts, but black, green, yellow, and gold were also used. Triglyphs were blue; metopes and stringcourses, as well as parts of the cornice, were red. Thus it may be seen that color was used to emphasize the various parts of the building.

A great deal of architectural decoration, both in relief and in the round, was painted in the conventional (not naturalistic) manner. Subject matter for sculpture was liberally taken from plant and animal life. Many of the motifs, such as the acanthus leaf and the lotus bud and flower, are still used today. Geometric patterns were also widely used and include nonrepresentational fret and mosaic patterns, all of which were brightly colored. The human figure was used for decoration and for both marble and bronze sculpture. Although there are few remaining examples, the statuary of the ancient Greeks was brightly colored, the marble figures being painted yellow, red, blue, and green. Sometimes stones of great value were used to represent eyes.

Because of the great need for containers for liquids such as honey and oil, pottery making became an important art, and, interestingly enough, much of the day-by-day life of Greece was used as subject matter in decorating this pottery. Occasionally geometric patterns were used, but many times a story is told with human and animal figures. Early pottery was purple and white; later it was glazed in black on reddish clay. The later pieces show figures and patterns of red on a black background. Refinements were constantly being made, and in the sixth and fifth centuries B.C., for instance, vases were produced which used the black on terra-cotta; panels not covered by black were painted with black figures.

Over the centuries, the Greeks developed a keen sense of refined beauty in which all the elements of a building were studied for balance, proportion, and harmony. Sculpture, carvings, and color were employed to heighten this refinement. Although Greece began to lose its political importance after the death of Alexander in 323 B.C., its architectural influence continued in other lands.

Rome

Although the civilizations of Greece and Italy developed about the same time, that of Greece developed more quickly, coming to its greatest height in the fifth and fourth centuries B.C. The Etruscans, culturally similar to the Greeks, probably emigrated from

Asia Minor and were in control of most of Italy. They lived in heavily fortified cities, and their homes were brightly decorated. However, the best of the Etruscan paintings that have come down to us were painted on the walls of chamber tombs. Unfortunately many of these were destroyed by atmospheric conditions once the tombs were opened. The subject matter of the tomb paintings included gay, lifelike scenes of banquets, sports, music, etc. These tombs, which only the wealthy could afford, were connected to the home of the family. Painting was not very often used on anything but walls, stone sarcophagi, and terra-cotta urns.

Of the wall paintings, the most important are from the Necropolis of Tarquinia. Here we find a series of paintings which date from the middle of the sixth century B.C. The subject matter is, for the most part, taken from Greek mythology, and human figures are painted in a shade of red upon a lightly colored background, horses in an off-white and red, trees brown, and leaves green, all in a very stylized fashion. Gradually the Greek influence waned, and Greek forms were recast and varied so that they became representative of the strength of the Roman Empire. Subjects included warriors, horses, flags, shields, etc., all contained between borders of ornament. Off-white backgrounds were sometimes used. Colors included black, brown, red, and a golden yellow.

Some large figure compositions showing gods and goddesses are painted with deep blue backgrounds and white, pinkish-red, and green clothing. They show a great deal of detail. Some paintings use warm flesh tones together with red and black, while others use flesh and warm tones for figures and clothing and green or white for the background. Still-life paintings also include the use of this complementary color scheme. Other still-life paintings use birds, snakes, and flowers painted in bright colors on dark, almost black, backgrounds.

Mosaics seem to have followed the same color pattern as the wall paintings, with flesh tones set against black and white and with the occasional use of a blue green. As time passed, the paintings and mosaics became more complicated in composition and more delicate in color.

The invading armies of Rome brought back with them many Greek works of art and many Greek artists. The Romans, masters of the more practical arts of building, seem to have been satisfied with the use of imported artists and imported works of art for the decoration of their great public buildings. Most of the color and texture of the public buildings, however, was obtained by the use of the materials themselves: marble, alabaster, porphyry, and jasper for walls, and marbles and mosaics for floors. There were also mural decorations in fresco.

What little we know about the paintings of these times we have obtained through a study of the works in Pompeii. Many were in small or private buildings that were preserved for centuries by the lava of Vesuvius which destroyed that city in A.D. 79. A great many decorative mural paintings were made between the second century B.C. and A.D. 80, and from this period we have numerous examples of Pompeian paintings. Walls were painted to imitate marble facing; friezes were painted; the artists seem to have struggled to cover the walls with architectural fantasies, perspectives, "outside" windows, and doors. Later painting seems to have used architectural scenes less often, and the walls were divided into many colored panels with carefully painted linear patterns containing human figures and animals. Backgrounds were yellow, red, green, and black. Information gathered during the excavations seems to indicate that the colors available to the artists of that period included a white made from pumice stone, a green earth pigment, blue, scarlet (pink), brown-red ochre, and a yellow ochre.

By A.D. 300, Rome, although visually still magnificent, had become decadent and its influence was soon to wane.

THE MEDIEVAL PERIOD

Constantine, by moving his capital to Byzantium (which he renamed Constantinople) in A.D. 330, divided the Roman Empire into two sections, East and West. Christianity, spreading from the eastern Mediterranean through Constantinople to Rome, produced many outstanding church buildings that varied in style according to location. In such lands as Persia, Egypt, Asia Minor, and Syria, Christian buildings followed somewhat the architectural traditions of these older civilizations, while in Rome they were influenced by existing Roman architecture. It was at powerful Constantinople, with its strategic location, that Roman and Eastern influences merged to become what we now term the Byzantine style. Western Europe, invaded by barbarians, now found itself amid the remains of the Roman imperial culture mixed with the primitive ideas of the invading hordes. Church building, lacking the strength and direct influence which the builders of churches in Rome had supplied, ground slowly to a halt. In the East and in Constantinople in particular, art and architecture began to be modified by such factors as the dislike of the early Christian for anything pagan, the Semitic dislike for the representation of sacred personages, and the influence of Islam, which set the stage for an image-destroying attitude that resulted in the use of architectural ornamentation employing geometric and floral motifs, the use of texture, and rich color. No single age has left us so many large, liberally decorated monuments—the decoration varying, of course, with location. Because of the development of mathematics in Egypt, those areas in contact with that country show a great deal of geometric ornament. In Rome pictorial treatment of wall and door surfaces continued as in earlier Italian architecture. The Romanesque church used polychromy for sculpture and also used mural painting. The Middle Ages, well known as a period of great stone sculpture, were also a great age of painting, especially great story-telling paintings. Textiles were used as well. In this period, walls, vaults, and the intrados of arches were frequently painted in a manner remindful of the ornamental bands of manuscript decoration.

Color was often rich in some parts of what is now France, and such colors as violet were used. In other parts of the same area, colors were lighter in tone and included red ochre, yellow ochre, black, white, and cinnabar. Green was rarely used, and blue was usually reserved for representations of the garments of Christ.

Recently the altarpiece in the Church of Ambierle, 60 miles northwest of Lyons, was restored. This Gothic church, dating from the end of the fifteenth century, contains beautiful examples of stained-glass windows, but the treasure is the altarpiece, 7 feet high and 9 feet long when closed and twice as long when open. Its sculptured fixed portion tells the story of the Crucifixion, while the movable panels are covered with portraits of the family of the donor and their patron saints. The carved figures are of walnut, available in the south central portion of France, and the case is of oak, used mainly in the north. It has not been definitely established whether this altarpiece is a Flemish or a Burgundian work of art.

The restoration of this altarpiece was undertaken by France's Direction des

Monuments Historiques. Broken pieces of the sculpture were meticulously restored, and delicate borings were made to find the original colors. Wherever colors were lacking, the artists proceeded by deduction and constantly referred to other similar works of that period. The carved figures of the main portion are in various shades of red, white, occasionally blue green, and brown, against the gilded tracery background. The painted panels show figures in costumes of red, yellow, and black, while the trompe-l'oeil statues on the outside are white in niches of crimson.

In Italy, the early painted pictures on wooden panels expressed the beauty of the Umbrian, Tuscan, and Sienese landscapes; they were often on parts of a chest, altar, or door. These brightly colored paintings were the forerunners of the modern painting. During the last part of the fourteenth century and the beginning of the fifteenth century, the brilliantly colored miniature landscapes depicted houses in pale yellow, coral, pink, and white, usually on backrounds of dark, olive-green hills.

Many examples of the art of this period can be seen in the famous collection at The Cloisters of New York's Metropolitan Museum of Art. The six tapestries representing The Hunt of the Unicorn are worthy of note because of the harmony in the use of the colors. The reds, yellows, blues, and orange are used dramatically to emphasize the white unicorn, and the green and blue-green foliage provides a subtle background to enhance the many details. It is regrettable that it has not been possible to establish without doubt whether these renowned works of art are of Flemish or French origin.

Other monuments to this great period in history include the Cathedral of Notre Dame at Chartres, started in 1150, Notre Dame in Paris, started in 1163, the Cathedral at Rouen, 1200, and Reims, 1211. In England, Salisbury Cathedral was constructed between 1220 and 1258, and Westminster Abbey was begun in 1250. The time, effort, and money of many men were expended in the beautification, including the coloring, of these religious structures.

THE RENAISSANCE

The Italian Renaissance

The Church, with its center in Rome, had become extremely powerful during the Medieval period, but with power came a decay in morality. This, combined with heavy taxation, set the stage for a reaction against the suppression of human emotion and thought. Color returned to buildings used by the living and was employed to express the enjoyment of life and nature. The Church, powerless to suppress further the interest in the works of antiquity took them for its own, and with them, classic color.

The wealthy merchants of Italy became patrons of the arts, and they built and decorated enormous palaces. These were decorated with painted frescoes, embroideries, and tapestries. The scenes used in the murals included antique ruins, religious and classic subjects, and often important happenings in the history of the patron's family. Often the colors in the murals determined the other room colors and the colors of accessories. Between 1400 and 1500, marble slabs were used in wall treatments and for trim, the field often being of one color, the moldings another. Gold was sometimes used on the capitals of columns and pilasters, as well as on ornamental cast plaster objects.

During the early part of the Renaissance, less wealthy merchants built smaller country villas. In these, expensive architectural forms were usually omitted, and richness was obtained inexpensively by painting imitation textiles, complete with folds, on sand-finished plaster walls. Wood-beamed ceilings were vividly striped with paint, and wood-paneled ceilings were often covered with arabesques, scenes, or ornament. Floors were often made with terrazzo and with colored or black-and-white marble and tile. Wherever economically feasible, the color of natural materials was used. Imitation painted "marble" dadoes, as well as sculptured, painted plaster forms, completed the artificial richness of the villas' interiors.

The furniture of the Renaissance, as well as its cabinetry, was most often made of walnut, and this rich brown wood was sometimes enriched by the use of small ivory inlaid patterns and by painted and gilded ornament.

Textiles used for upholstery and draperies were usually made of silk, their patterns being large and colorful. Dress velvets, made in Genoa, were often used for loose cushions and for the upholstery of small pieces of furniture. It is interesting to note that the Italian Renaissance architect (artisan) took the size of a room into consideration when selecting colors. Large rooms received strong colors, smaller rooms softer shades. If neutral-colored plaster walls were used, accessories and draperies were usually brightly colored. In addition to natural colors, the colors used in ancient Greece, Rome, and Egypt continued to be used. These were changed and modified, however, so that, for instance, the scarlet used in ancient Greece became a yellower "pompeii red." Bluish reds appeared. Some gold became rich golden yellow and reddish browns became yellower browns. Generally speaking, the colors used in this period were brown, blue green, a medium greenish blue, a brilliant medium red, and, of course, gold.

This was the period that saw the construction of St. Peter's in Rome (1506–1626) and such other masterpieces as the Gardens of the Villa d'Este at Tivoli (1549). It was the age of Michelangelo Buonarroti (1475–1564), Luca della Robbia (1400–1482), Leonardo da Vinci (1452–1519), Raphael (1483–1520), and Titian (1477–1576). It was, of course, an age of color.

The Flemish Renaissance

While the Renaissance was maturing in Italy in the fifteenth century, its effect began to be felt in all parts of Europe. Each area changed it as it assimilated it. Flanders, a trading station and typical medieval city, was a meeting place for people from all parts of the world at that time. Because of its wealth, art developed at a great pace, and public buildings and private houses were frequently adorned with statuary and carved work, much of which was gilded and colored. Windows were often made of stained glass, and paintings and tapestries were in abundance. One of the greatest contributions made to the arts by Flanders was its establishment of guilds. The painters' guild, for instance, taught the necessary skills to apprentices, who later became journeymen, then masters. The guild obtained commissions for its members and inspected their work, passing upon the honesty of materials and workmanship.

The buildings of Flanders in the fourteenth and fifteenth centuries were Gothic in design and therefore lacked large wall surfaces. The paintings, consequently, were mostly miniatures and illuminations, and the only large-scale use of color occurred in the making of windows. In the fifteenth century, however, large paintings were executed by the van Eyck brothers (Jan, 1385–1440, and Hubert, 1370–1426). Their works, painted in oils, included brilliant colors as well as gold and black. The colors have held up extraordinarily well. Although they did not invent the medium of oil, the van Eycks' efforts produced better results than had been obtained previously. Tapestries, too, grew larger and more complicated; they became more brilliant and colorful as the invention of new dyes produced intermediate tones.

The English Renaissance

Because England was a seafaring nation, color was liberally borrowed from many lands. During the Early Renaissance period (1500–1660) color was limited to the use of stained glass and several kinds of wood, including oak. Those walls which were not paneled were sometimes covered with rough-finish plaster. Exposed ceiling beams were sometimes carved and painted, as were plaster ceiling patterns.

During the reigns of Henry VIII and Elizabeth, trading ships brought Chinese pottery and porcelains, Turkish rugs, and hand-painted tree-of-life cottons from India. Lighting fixtures were of brass, silver, and wrought iron. Long velvet hangings were frequently used around beds to ensure warmth and privacy.

During the English Restoration (1660–1689) the walls of most rooms continued to be paneled. The wood, walnut or oak, was usually left in its natural state but was sometimes marbleized. Less expensive woods such as pine and fir were often grained to imitate walnut. Olive-wood ornamentation and moldings were often gilded. In the absence of wood paneling, walls were covered with damask or velvet. English and French tapestries were hung in places of importance. Parquet floors of ebony and oak were used, and over these were placed Oriental rugs. It was during this period that Sir Christopher Wren's St. Paul's Cathedral (1668–1670) and St. Mary-le-Bow Church (1680) were constructed in London.

Wall-hung framed paintings and mirrors appeared in the eighteenth century. Colored marbles such as white Siena and dark green verde antique were frequently used for fireplace mantels. Natural-finish knotty pine was used for wall panels, and flock wallpaper, an inexpensive substitute for Italian cut velvet, was introduced. Wallpapers imitating marble and tapestry were also used, and by the middle of the century scenic and pictorial Chinese-inspired papers began to appear. Upholstery included leather and textiles.

The reign of William and Mary (1689–1702) is known as the Age of Walnut, while mahogany was introduced as a cabinet wood during the reigns of Queen Anne (1702–1714) and George I (1714–1727). Furniture was sometimes painted with Chinese or Japanese lacquer. The last part of the eighteenth century and the beginning of the nineteenth are sometimes called the Age of Satinwood because of the introduction of this wood by George Hepplewhite.

The manufacture of colorful and decorative fabrics such as damasks, brocades, velvets, crewel embroideries, brocatelles, and needlepoint reached a high point of development in the skill of the Huguenots, who were forced to leave France because of religious persecution. During the end of the seventeenth century chintz began to be used decoratively.

After the middle of the eighteenth century, plaster often took the place of wood paneling for rooms, and while occasionally these walls were painted a pale color, they were just as often painted white.

The period of the Late Renaissance (1750–1830) in England, including Middle Georgian (1750–1770), Late Georgian (1770–1810), Regency (1810–1820), and Victorian (1837–1901), produced artists whose influence survives today. Thomas Chippendale, George Hepplewhite, Thomas Sheraton, and the Adam brothers (Robert, 1728–1792, and James, 1730–1794) were responsible for the development of some of the finest rooms of the period. They strove for a unity of effect, designing all parts to blend into the whole, both exterior and interior. The rooms were large and formal and were greatly influenced by classic forms found during the excavations then going on at Pompeii and Herculaneum. Wood-paneled walls gave way to plaster decorated with plaster ornament, and moldings. The walls were often painted in pale tones of green, ivory, gray, yellow, and blue; the deeper colors were sparingly used. The Adams used many different shades of green. White marble or plaster figures were often set in niches, crystal chandeliers glittered in the ceilings, and furniture was covered in satins and damasks. The refinement and dignity of these rooms are a high point in design.

It was not long, however, before this style declined into the Regency period with its heavy hand and heavy colors. The development of machines to take over the work of the craftsmen began. During the Victorian period industrialized England produced an incredible variety of gingerbread ornament and objects. All available space was covered with objects of every sort. Colors were most often heavy and dull, with mauve and purples very popular. Although cream and buff appeared occasionally, by the end of the period, popularly referred to as "The Mauve Decade," there was a wide use of depressing taupes, grays, and browns.

The French Renaissance

At a time when the Renaissance was beginning in Italy, France was consolidating its country after numerous invasions. Gothic art and architecture were declining, and France was ready for a change. The rulers of France, beginning with Charles VIII (r. 1483–1498), were aware of the richness of Renaissance art in Italy and contrasted it unfavorably with their own relatively barren castles. Wars between Italy and France, and subsequent "victories" by France, resulted in the importation of Italian craftsmen. The Renaissance in France dates approximately from the reign of Francis I (1515–1547), who was held prisoner in Italy after a military defeat. During his incarceration he became aware of the rich colors and interior designs of the Italian buildings and brought this interest back to France with him. Henry II (r. 1547–1559) married Catherine de Médici, who continued the introduction of the Italian arts to France. Henry IV (r. 1589–1610) was instrumental in creating religious tolerance in France, and this attracted many Protestant craftsmen from the Low Countries.

Under Louis XIV (r. 1643–1715) France attained a high level of decorative splendor, and French taste was soon accepted as the standard throughout Europe. However, political mistakes in addition to huge sums spent on costly displays, parties, and amusements, depleted the French treasury and impoverished the people of France. The regency established during the childhood of Louis XV (r. 1715–1774) could do little to improve the economic condition of France, and when he came to the throne, he joined in the luxurious and extravagant life of the court. Louis XVI, weak and impulsive, ruled at a time when France had lost its American colonies and the respect of the rest of Europe. Several years after the French Revolution began, he was executed. The subsequent Directorate (1795–1799) did little to enrich the art of the country, and it was not until Napoleon was proclaimed consul that further progress was made in improving the arts. The aristocracy, who had been responsible for the luxury and refinement of French architecture and interiors, had fled to other countries, and during Napoleon's empire a much less sophisticated style appeared for a much less sophisticated clientele. The Empire period lasted from 1804 to 1814.

The interior architectural spaces of the French Renaissance were large and dark, and walls were usually hung with Gothic tapestries or painted in patterns. Some Gothic wood paneling was used, and structural ceiling beams were often painted. Under Henry II the coffered ceiling panel came into use, and marble-patterned papers were used on walls. During the reigns of Henry IV and Louis XIII, palace rooms became larger and more formal. As the people turned away from the church toward more worldly interests, châteaus and civic buildings received more attention. Wood wall panels became larger and moldings heavier. The fields of these panels were often painted with patterns borrowed from Spain and Italy. They were almost never left in a natural finish. Moldings were grained and gilded on an off-white background. Floors were occasionally of oak parquet or black-and-white marble and were sometimes covered with aubusson tapestry rugs or savonnerie pile rugs in colors that harmonized with the rooms in which they were used. Ceiling coves were occasionally painted with ornament, and the centers of ceilings were often painted with scenes depicting angels and other heavenly beings. Although the rooms of the early Renaissance châteaus did not contain much furniture, that which was used was heavily built and Gothic in feeling. Walnut, oak, and ebony were used for variation in color. Finer furniture was carved, or inlaid with woods of contrasting colors or with bronze, which was sometimes set with semi-precious stones. Upholstery included needlework, velvet, leather, and damask.

It was during the reign of Louis XIV, who determined to make his court the most imposing in Europe, that work was started on Versailles, with its formal gardens and magnificent fountains. Leaders in the fields of architecture, sculpture, painting, and the other arts, as well as craftsmen to execute their designs, were gathered from all parts of Europe to carry this program forward. The conception and execution were of great formality with an extravagance of detail. Rooms were large, with large-scale furniture; curves formed by the compass were used abundantly. Furniture frames, heavily carved, were of ebony, oak, sycamore, chestnut, walnut, and other, more exotic, woods. Marble was a favorite for table tops. Upholstery included damasks, velvets, leather, needlepoint, cane, and tapestry. Although colors such as blue and gray were inclined to be bright and strong there was a gradual development of the lighter tones of gray green, gray blue, beige, and pale cream.

As women began to take a more active part in life at court, their influence was also felt in decoration. Furniture, colors, and other aspects of interior design became thinner, lighter, and more effeminate. When her influence became very strong during the reign of Louis XV, Madame de Pompadour spent a great deal of time furthering the arts. It was through her efforts that royal societies and patronage for the porcelain factory at Sèvres were advanced, and it was at Sèvres that new chemicals were developed to produce the gold, rose, and king's blue for which this factory became famous. Madame de Pompadour also became interested in Oriental art, and designs with Chinese motifs were developed for use in interiors. It is interesting to note that Chinese hand-painted wallpapers of the time could be imported for less than French artisans charged for making them. Wallpaper was so admired by the middle classes that facilities for its manufacture were set up by Jean Papillon at the end of the seventeenth century.

Textile patterns used for draperies became smaller around this time, and printed cottons in large repeats in red, eggplant, green, and blue, printed on white grounds by the hand-blocked process, became popular. Colors became pale, and neutral hues were used.

Marquetry was very popular in furniture; and in addition to oak, cherry, apple, mahogany, and pear, tulipwood, violetwood, kingwood, and amaranth were used. All these woods were decorated with gold ormolu. In many cases, furniture was also painted in light shades of cream, sky blue, gray, rose, and apricot. Furniture was upholstered in cane, taffeta, brocade, needlepoint, damask, leather, and *toile de Jouy*.

During the reign of Louis XVI, paneling was not usually carved, and the panels were often painted a plain color or decorated with landscapes and the like. Sometimes textiles were applied. Wallpaper was also used to cover wood panels on plaster walls in simple rooms. Except in the most elaborate rooms, ceilings were merely painted, but in the formal rooms they were decorated to imitate the sky. Furniture was made of mahogany and often painted. Japanese black-and-gold lacquer was substituted for the brighter Chinese types. The colors of materials used for upholstery tended to be light and feminine. Marie Antoinette used smaller rooms as a means of escape from the astonishingly large *salons* of the time. Although the Petit Trianon (1762–1768) was built in the gardens of Versailles during the reign of Louis XV, it has become more closely associated with the name of Marie Antoinette and the trend toward decoration on a simpler scale. Pastel shades of green, yellow brown, pink, chartreuse, and gold became popular.

During the reign of Napoleon, two young architects, Percier and Fontaine, whose taste resembled that of the Adam-period designers in England, set the style of the day. Walls were not often paneled with wood but were hung with wallpaper or textiles and sometimes painted with Pompeian figures. Drapery fabrics were in heavy silk with strongly contrasting colors. Emerald greens, royal purples, brilliant yellows and blues, and wine red formed the spot patterns, which featured victory shields, bees, rosettes, and the letter N. The cabinetmakers attempted to alter their styles, but although they managed to produce furniture of good lines and proportions, economic factors lowered the quality of construction and the amount of ornament was decreased. Gradually the pieces became heavy and ungraceful. After Napoleon's defeat at Waterloo, the Empire style slowly declined and was finally destroyed by machine production.

THE UNITED STATES

At a time when travel, even for short distances, was exceedingly difficult, settlers came to America from England and developed colonies in Virginia and New England. Unquestionably, the Virginians were different in background from the New Englanders. Many of those who settled in Virginia had lived with the highly developed color schemes that they knew in England. The New England colonials were, for the most part, from a less affluent background. It is only natural that more highly developed and elaborate homes were built in the South, where land had been given by royal grant and where luxuries could be imported. In the early days at least, the less wealthy people of New England, who had a harsher climate to deal with, lived with the bare necessities of life. These did not include elaborate homes or richly furnished interiors.

In New England walls were for the most part white or off-white. Colorful carpet in patterns of oranges, whites, and greens covered the floors. Bedspreads were white or colored. Printed cottons were used for upholstery. The colors of these cottons included mustard yellows, reds, white, and combinations of green, red, and yellow. During the pre-Revolutionary period, when Captain's Houses were very popular, color in New England became heavier in tone and patterns were used. Cotton fabrics with off-white backgrounds were often seen patterned with muted golds and with yellow flowers and green leaves. By and large, the period is marked by a certain practical charm owing to its correct use of color and texture.

Between 1666 and 1720, political conditions in England quieted down, and the American settlers were able to concentrate on enriching their surroundings. By the beginning of the eighteenth century it was obvious that the colonies in America were becoming successful, and this drew additional settlers, including craftsmen such as cabinetmakers and carpenters.

The Georgian look that gave the eighteenth century an elegant quality was greatly influenced by the work of Sir Christopher Wren (1632–1723). It is said that many of the designs of Colonial Williamsburg and of such plantation houses as Carter's Grove were developed by him. The colors used in interiors became stronger. At Carter's Grove, one finds large-patterned red and white draperies, red and golden-yellow walls with bright red curtains and upholstery, and red walls with white trim. In the smaller rooms the colors were more muted: grayish wainscots and trim were set off with red curtains. Often upper walls were white with brightly colored curtains. Often, too, the trim was white, and subdued blue and white wallpaper was used. In another interesting combination, walls and trim were painted a soft, pale gold, with chair seats a bright golden yellow to set off the mahogany furniture and oriental carpet. The dark mahogany furniture and the deep reddish-brown floor completed the picture. Woodwork was most often painted a color contrasting with the walls, but occasionally they were both the same color.

By the middle of the eighteenth century, the Colonies had developed to the point where they could be more heavily taxed by England, and this precipitated the Revolution. The period following the Revolution was one in which certain men, such as Franklin, Hamilton, Jefferson, and Washington, who prided themselves in their knowledge of the arts, not only began to construct more elaborate structures with refined interiors, but, by their example, encouraged the people in the colonies to again look toward Europe for architectural examples.

By the end of the eighteenth and the beginning of the nineteenth centuries, a number of fine examples of post-Colonial architecture began to appear. The inspiration came in great part from ancient Greece and Rome. Although the doors and trim of many buildings of this era were white, the walls were often covered with elaborate paintings and with wallpaper in flowered or diamond patterns; and the rugs, which had been quiet in pattern and color, suddenly became larger-patterned and used brilliant pinks, blues, and yellows. Often, too, the colors of the draperies were bright. In the beginning, New England colors were quieter and more closely related than in later periods.

Williamsburg's interiors were notable because of their restraint and good taste. Few colors were used, but these were employed to accentuate the correctly detailed classic interior spaces. Among the papers of William Allason, a late-eighteenth-century wholesale merchant of Falmouth, Virginia, we find an invoice for such items as linseed oil, fig blue, one barrel of lampblack, one cask of spanish-brown paint, one cask of white lead, and prussian blue. While pigments, especially the ochres and reds, were used in their pure form in many instances, many different hues were obtained by mixing the pigments and by introducing lampblack. All details of these interiors were elegant, and the use of colors was carefully limited: one high color note was used, and all other color elements in the room were subservient to it. Great attention was given to the correct proportion of each color and to the proper amount and disposition of each. In effect, the rooms became three-dimensional paintings.

It is natural that color used in the United States should reflect the national origins of its settlers. Since most of this country's original settlers came from England, early color was indeed English, but even here there was a difference depending upon locale, background of population, and affluence. The settlers in Williamsburg were familiar with the fine English architecture of that time and reproduced it to the best of their considerable ability. Paint colors were made with imported pigments, and many delightful hues were mixed from them. Northern English settlers, less affluent, had to be content with little or no color. Similarly, but on a much smaller scale, the Dutch, French, Swedes, and Germans influenced the areas in which they settled, each group using color in the same way that it had been used in their part of Europe.

The post-Colonial period, particularly the end of the eighteenth and beginning of the nineteenth centuries, produced many fine Greco-Roman buildings in the United States. English colors, together with some from France and some borrowed from ancient times, were popular. A rather bleak period followed, lasting roughly until the Centennial Exposition which was held in Philadelphia in 1876. This event coincided with a desire for rich surroundings on the part of many *nouveau riche* in New York, Newport, Chicago, and elsewhere. In order to obtain an aura of culture as quickly as possible, they commissioned their architects to build imitation châteaus and palaces which were copied from those in Europe. Although many celebrated edifices arose, the ordinary individual contented himself with the fussy, ornate, and tasteless style of the Victorian period. Colors continued to be drab and monotonous; cream and buff were most popular. Upholstery and fabrics in burgundy and bright blue were popular.

With the twentieth century came World War I, the airplane, Frank Lloyd Wright, the automobile and the movement to the suburbs, motion pictures, the International Style, the Great Depression, World War II, the Korean War, and the war in Vietnam, all of which affected the daily lives of the entire population and influenced the manner in which people lived. It was not until the end of World War II that tremendous changes evolved in architecture and the arts to bring us to the challenging situation of today.

THE ORIENT

India

Although there are many different peoples and many different climates in India, religion seems to have overcome these differences and to have determined India's architecture and use of architectural color. While national forces were changing with various religious pressures, foreign influences from the West also made themselves felt. Invasions by the Greeks under Alexander and later by the Sassanian Persians left their marks. During the fifth century, a high degree of excellence in the fields of sculpture and painting was achieved in buildings which were essentially meeting halls. Because most of the early meeting halls were apparently built of wood, they are no longer in existence. In about the year 1001, the Muhammadans had invaded India from the east; by 1526 they had established the Mogul empire, and this was the ruling force in India until the English, Dutch, and French arrived in the seventeenth century. English rule was established in 1818.

Rock-cut churches, temples, and monasteries, and buildings such as the Taj Mahal (which is built of white marble inlaid with precious stones in floral patterns) permit us to see the exquisite use of color by the artisans of this land. Wall paintings of the eighteenth century exhibit the importance of contour; figures, for instance, are suggested but are painted flat. Although no paintings from the middle of the seventh century to the eighteenth century seem to have survived, samples of cotton fabric have come down to us. Weaving was one of the most important crafts in India, and the textiles served not only as material for clothing, but for bedspreads, hangings, and other furnishings. The word "chintz" was derived from the native name for this material. These fabrics were decorated by printing and painting. Sometimes colors were painted by hand, while colors such as blue were dyed because this was more permanent. Brilliant colors were often used in the arts of India as well as in its architecture and these were adapted to use by Westerners.

China

The people of ancient China were interested in natural phenomena such as rain, stars, sky, and wind, and their religion was based upon forces of nature. The individual was subservient to the family, and the customs of previous generations later became the law. Just as the individual was a part of an unbroken chain over the centuries, so each type of architecture, together with its colors, remained constant. This constancy is due to the ritualistic and symbolic use of color. For example, royal buildings were roofed in yellow tile, yellow being the color of the royal family. Other tile colors, such as green or blue, were used according to the rank or social status of the owner. Columns, beams, soffits of roof overhangs, and the interiors of these buildings were carved and richly painted with vermilion and gold. Parts of such areas were often lacquered.

One may again see the importance of color in ritual in the Temple of Heaven, Peiping, built during the eighteenth century. The tiles of the temple are a deep cobalt to represent the color of heaven. During spring ceremonies, blue was used throughout the service. There were blue porcelain accessories and blue glass windows; the worshipers themselves wore blue to cast a hue over the entire proceeding. In similar fashion, Buddhist pagodas were sometimes faced with glazed tiles in yellow, deep reddish blue, green, and red. Wall paintings, done in a flat, two-dimensional manner, were painted as frescoes, panels, and scrolls. Pictures as we know them did not exist, and the panels and wall paintings were not on display constantly but were brought out for special occasions.

Chinese black ink was used for painting as well as for writing. Paintings in this medium were made on silk and were characterized by their delicacy and soft appearance. Mountain scenery was a favorite subject and was beautifully and creatively composed. The mood was usually calm and peaceful. It is interesting to note that certain formulas, protected by custom, were used even here. Mountains could be drawn in sixteen different ways, each of which was fixed in its characteristics.

Of the minor arts, the best bronzes were made in the early periods. Jade was used for personal ornaments, bells, and decoration. Ceramics were at various times given a greenish glaze or painted with brown, green, and yellow glaze. The color of the ceramic pottery varies according to period. During the Ming dynasty (1368–1644) temple vases were painted with a black background with gold chrysanthemums. During the K'ang-Hsi period (1662–1722) vases were painted bright yellow, green, and brown. In the same period, one may also see french ultramarine blue, white, green, coral, and gold. During the last sixty years of the eighteenth century, coral, blue green, pink, terra-cotta, and lavender came into use. The vases were in many different shapes and sizes. Westerners are perhaps most familiar with celadon, a soft green color. This color may have been used as an imitation of expensive jade.

Japan

Although Shintoism, whose main tenets are an awe and thankfulness before the forces of nature, has long played an important part in the life of Japan, the most important element in its Japanese culture was Buddhism. By the sixth century, Buddhism had changed Chinese thought and culture, and had passed its version of them on to Japan. At first, the art of Japan reflected that of China, India, and Korea. Later, however, these tendencies were assimilated. Buddhistic influence came from China in three waves: the first during the reign of Empress Suiko (593–628) in the Asuka period (552–645), the second from Tang China (618–907) during the Nara period in Japan (710–794), and the third from Sung China (960–1280) in the Kamakura (1185–1333) and Ashikagon (1338–1573) periods.

While Japan was absorbing these influences, its political power was slowly taken over by barons who set up a military feudalism. Later, the masses had more political importance, and differences of religion were tolerated. As Buddhism weakened, a democratic art began to develop.

Japanese architecture has always reflected a deep-seated love of nature, and a fondness for and understanding of wood, the chief available building material. Early Buddhist temples and monasteries imitated similar large Chinese buildings, and the structural parts of these temples were painted with an orange-type vermilion which is now frequently called "chinese red." The exterior walls were made of plaster painted white and sliding shoji screens. The interiors of the Buddhist monastery were very colorful. A statute of Buddha, painted in gold, was covered by a great canopy; the timbers were painted with blue, green, vermilion, and gold, and sometimes lacquered. Later, similar structures became lighter in proportion, and exteriors were of natural weathered wood. The interiors were richly treated, and the ceilings were covered with black lacquer and inlaid with mother-of-pearl, ivory, and silver. Much of the structure below was also in natural wood with portions decorated in chinese red and gold. The whole three-dimensional composition formed a magnificent background for those who used the building.

When built for the shoguns, large buildings such as Nijo Castle (1603) were enriched by magnificent and colorful wall paintings and shoji screens consisting of several hinged panels. The backgrounds of most of these paintings and screens were painted with gold dust, and the scenes painted on them included birds, animals, and landscapes. Although each composition was complete on the panel upon which it was painted, it was also part of a total composition of several panels. For example, a rock painted on one panel of a shoji screen continued on to the next. Only the great artists were allowed to do this work. As in Chinese paintings, large areas and many relatively unimportant elements are omitted from each picture. For example, in a four-panel composition at Nijo Castle, dominance is given to two white-and-green birds perched on top of a colorful, but basically gray, rock. Adjacent panels contain only a continuation of the rock on the left side and a pink flower with green leaves on the right. At the top corner of the right panel, however, green foliage of a large pine tree projects slightly into the panel, while a small portion of the trunk of the pine tree occupies only a small corner of the fourth panel. The trunk and large branch occupy two larger panels above. The colors of these paintings are subtle: the pine foliage is a muted bluish green, rocks are gray with tones of green and red, and the tail feathers of one of the birds is a golden vermilion. Other panels have golden-yellow tigers, slate-blue water, and deep green foliage. Wall panels are separated by wide bands of black lacquer and gold, and shojis are edged with narrow bands of black-lacquered wood. Natural-colored cedar timbers divide the panels above.

The Japanese home, whether large or small, achieves its charm by simple means. The interior of the home is united with the natural world outside by opening shojis onto a view of the garden. Vista is important. Colors of materials which are an integral part of the structure are subtle and are those colors found in nature—natural cedar, blue-gray tile, and stucco. Golden-yellow tatami mats are edged with brown for people of the lowest class or with black for the next highest class; they are patterned if for use in buildings occupied by people of great importance. There is little furniture, since the Japanese prefer to sit cross-legged on the floor at low tables, which are usually chinese red or deep mahogany in color.

The highest color note of such a room is located on the *tokonoma*, or raised area, which is used as a shrine. Here one will find a painted scroll, with, for instance, a gray border and picturing a gray and red rooster and blond wood, all framed with a narrow black-lacquered frame. In front of the scroll, flowers of an appropriate color, arranged to complement the entire composition, are placed in a vase or bowl. The tokonoma scroll and flowers are changed for various events and seasons. Interestingly enough, one's guest is seated with his back to the tokonoma, since it is there that he will look most important and honored!

Although color seems to have been sparingly used in dwellings, it must be remembered that the Japanese are constantly aware of it, if not preoccupied with it. Thousands of years of excellent and colorful Japanese art may be seen in the many museums both in Japan and around the world. Most of it has been commendably preserved. The subject matter varies, but includes buildings; war, rituals; such visitors to Japan as the Portuguese, Dutch, and Americans; daily life; and, of course, the many Japanese rulers. Colors include green, red, gold, blue, chinese red, yellow, and black and white. In all cases the total effect is a calm understatement of the subject. In its highest degree of perfection, Japanese art reaches the exquisite state of design referred to as *shibui*.

Colors used in the various periods of human history depended upon their availability. Stone Age man used minerals such as lime, ochre, manganese, and red iron for pigments. For vehicles he used blood, fats, and milk. In addition to these colors, white and black were used by the Stone Age painters in North Africa. The Egyptian painter used clay, mud, and plant juices. The colors for murals were given an adhesive quality by the use of animal glue, wax, and resins, and those used for vase painting were mixed with casein, egg, rubber, and honey. The Greeks and Etruscans were influenced by the Egyptian painters and used similar materials, adding a few of their own. The painting of interiors was done with tempera (containing pigment and egg, and sometimes rubber, milk, or glue). Chinese and Japanese painters used water-soluble pigments when painting on silk, and lacquer when painting on wood. Indian artists used opaque pigments. Pompeian paintings were made with a palette which included a lake-type pink, brown-red ochre, yellow ochre, veronese-green earth, blue, and white.

True paint is a mixture of a pigment with a vehicle. The fluid portion, the vehicle, carries small pieces of pigment in suspension and binds them, by oxidation and hardening, to the painted surface. "Oil paint" is a paint in which the vehicle is a drying oil (usually linseed oil). Oil paints have been used for protective or decorative purposes since the twelfth century.

Pigments may be classified according to source, hue, or chemical composition. Pigments come from various sources—earth, minerals, vegetables, and animals. In addition, organic and inorganic pigments are made synthetically.

Earth pigments include the ochres, siennas, umbers, and green earth. Ochres vary from yellow through red to brown. Italian ochres which contain more than 50 to 70 percent ferric oxide are called siennas because the largest deposit of this material is at Siena, Italy. Umber is a natural earth color. The most common type, which comes from Cyprus, is known as raw turkey umber and is a warm reddish brown with a green cast. When it is roasted, it turns reddish brown and is called burnt umber. Vandyke brown comes from a rich brown earth mined near Cologne, Germany. Green earth, also called veronese or tyrolese green, is made from earth rich in iron oxide. Today all earth colors are manufactured synthetically and therefore inexpensively.

A number of pigments exist as minerals in nature. Cinnabar (sometimes called vermilion) was used in ancient China, Greece, and Rome. In Greece and Rome it was so expensive that only the wealthy could afford to use it In Rome, the amount of raw ore that was imported for processing was limited by law to about 2,000 pounds annually. During the eighth century A.D., an Arabian chemist named Geber discovered a way to produce cinnabar synthetically. The mass production of synthetic cinnabar began about 1785.

Blue azurite (mountain blue) and green malachite (mountain green) are copper minerals that were used in paintings in the Orient and in the West until the end of the Renaissance. Natural ultramarine blue was made of lapis lazuli, a semiprecious crystalline mineral. Although it was used for jewelry more than 5,000 years ago, it seems not to have been used as a pigment before the beginning of the sixth century. In 1828 an artificial ultramarine was produced and, despite its inferior quality, was more widely used because of its lower cost.

Natural white earths such as chalk, kaolin, barites, and china clay are not usable for mixing with oil because they are not opaque. Instead, today's whites are made of white lead, titanium white, and zinc white.

Of the yellows, chrome yellow, made from lead salt and chromate, was used in the nineteenth century and is still used as a tinting color in today's interior paints. Cadmium yellow ranges in shade from lemon to orange to yellow ochre.

Cadmium red, made of selenium and cadmium sulfite, is brighter and bluer than cinnabar.

A number of green colors, such as verdigris, usually made of some form of copper, were used in ancient times. Others, such as Scheele's green and emerald green, both of which contain arsenic, were used in the eighteenth and nineteenth centuries. About the middle of the nineteenth century anhydrous chromium oxide began to be manufactured commercially, and from it were made the chrome oxide greens, which are olive in shade.

Egyptian blue was made of powdered green glass, but it was difficult to apply, and when prussian blue was discovered in 1704, this largely took its place. Cobalt blue and cerulean blue, both chemically obtained, were first sold during the nineteenth century.

A great many blacks have been available to mankind. Lampblack, made of the soot formed by earthenware oil lamps, was used in China as long ago as 1500 B.C. Bistre, a brownish black, is made by burning beechwood; vine black by burning grape husks. Bone black and ivory black are made by charring bones. It should be noted that each type of black has its own cast: some are bluish, some brownish, some grayish, and some deep black. According to its own qualities, each black will therefore modify or change the color to which it is added.

Madder lake, a red, was formerly made by extracting a substance from the roots of the madder plant. Depending upon the conditions of manufacture, the color varied from pink to purple. Now a more stable madder lake is made from pure synthetic alizarin.

A number of other plants, such as persian berries (yellow and green), safflower (red), foxglove (yellow and red), and brasil wood, were once used to make green, yellow, and red lakes. Carmine, a crimson red used in Europe since the middle of the sixteenth century, is made from female cochineal insects. A number of other colors, used mostly for water-color painting, were made from such materials as the leaves of certain trees, fruit, and the ink bag of the cuttlefish (sepia).

Since about 1850 most dyes and pigments have been made synthetically. Although these dyes were at first not very lightfast, constant work has made them very permanent. This permanence is due largely to the discovery in 1935 of such phthalocyanine dyes as heliogen green and heliogen blue. Other fast colors include lithol red, permanent red, and sunfast red. Needless to say, artificially made dyes and pigments can be produced less expensively and in greater quantities than those made from natural materials. In fact, modern dyes for fabrics are superior in many ways to those made with the natural materials mentioned above. They have a high penetrating power and brightness of shade when this is desired; they are lightfast and may be easily cleaned. Improvements in quality and constancy and the development of new shades are made possible by the use of photomicrography with infrared light. New fabrics present new problems of dyeing, but these are constantly being solved by dye chemists. Colored fabrics, therefore, are more readily available to the masses today.

Gone is the dependence upon formulas handed down from father to son. Similarly, with the fantastic improvement in transportation, dyes and pigments are available to all, regardless of location. In addition, the use of color in other man-made products of construction, including tile, concrete, porcelain, aluminum, vinyl, and plastic, has advanced beyond all expectations in recent years.

SOCIOLOGICAL FACTORS

At the end of the nineteenth century, when the new moneyed aristocracy in the United States commissioned architects to build showplaces copied from those in Europe, many architects found it expeditious to study in Europe—particularly inasmuch as schools of architecture in the United States were, at that time, either nonexistent or basically schools of engineering. In sharp contrast, the Ecole des Beaux Arts at that time was the keeper of good taste, and Americans clamored to go there to study. By 1870, interest in architectural education in the United States had begun to develop. A number of books on home decoration were produced, and a few schools of art and architecture were formed. Subsequent years have seen them develop and multiply, until today, thanks to our many schools of architecture and interior design, many fine designers are supplied to the market each year.

Today, because of our mass media, particularly architectural and interior-design magazines, there is a greater mass understanding than ever before of the problems of interior design and, therefore, of color. Tastes change and vary, and styles wax and wane. Colors are either "in" or "not in" this year, but whatever else may be said, a broad interest in color exists such as the world has never before seen.

Taste is a personal matter, but our achitects and interior designers are its custodians. There are pressures, some natural and others artificial, which cause changes in color styles. Newspaper and magazine articles strongly suggest "colors of the month" or "year" for the homemaker, and these trends are accepted without question by many. It is interesting to the author that in the average homemaker's attempt to be individualistic, she conforms to a pattern and literally wears this year's color as a uniform. Although the homemaker can change the colors of her home as often as the budget will allow, buildings of a less personal nature must be color-designed for greater permanence. Public, industrial, and commercial structures must be studied carefully, and the many principles which are discussed in this book can be used to obtain more lasting results. While fluctuation and variation can be endured in a domestic environment, it is the task of today's designers to keep this trend in check in other buildings. Certainly no one would want to return to the austerity of Victorian or other times which dictated that walls be green, cream, peach, or whatever. Continued education in the use of color can develop an appreciation of its pleasures and advantages in everyone. The correct use of color in our public, commercial, and industrial buildings will further the education of the general public, and this must be the goal of today's designers.

chapter two

COLOR
THEORY AND
COLOR DESIGN

COLOR AND LIGHT

MANY theories have been advanced to explain color. The Illuminating Engineering Society *IES Lighting Handbook* says: "Color is considered to be a mental phenomenon which is evoked by light striking the back of the eye after passing through the ocular media." Most authorities agree that objects themselves do not have color, but that the color of an object is determined by its relative ability to absorb light rays. Because objects do not absorb the same quantity of light at each wave length, different colors are produced. When light strikes an object, it penetrates the surface somewhat. The extent of penetration and absorption depends upon the texture of the object. If an object absorbs all colors except red, red rays are reflected to the eye, and we call the object red. White light is a mixture of all colors. These colors may be seen when sunlight striking the curved surfaces of raindrops is spread into a rainbow. The same effect may be obtained by passing a narrow beam of light through a glass prism (see Figure 2.1).

White surfaces reflect all colors, absorbing none. Black surfaces, on the other hand, do not reflect colors, but absorb them. Thus black is the complete lack of light and color.

These basic facts are only a small part of the body of fascinating information about color and light amassed by men of science. But even in the world of science, different aspects of color concern different disciplines. For instance, the chemist may identify a color by a curved ink line produced by a spectrophotometer; the physicist might add to the curved ink line another curve corresponding to certain aspects of the light

FIG. 2.1 *Refraction of light through a glass prism*

source (that sends out energy which is then reflected off the sample); and the colorimetrist may take into account the relation between the visual response of a standard observer and the so-called stimulus aspects of the object.[1]

The psychologist, the artist, the architect, and the interior designer believe that certain other aspects of color must be considered. The appearance of color for them depends on viewing conditions, the surrounding objects or areas, the sizes and relative positions of objects, and the adaptive state of the viewer. It is for these reasons that for the purpose of this discussion we shall consider color as not merely reflection, but as an entity in itself, with its own properties.

Properties of Color

Color may be described as having three outstanding properties: hue, value, and intensity. Hue is the name of the color, such as blue, which differentiates it from another color, such as green. Value designates the brightness of a color, that is, whether the color is light or dark. Intensity, or chroma, denotes the extent to which the hue is free from any white constituent. The "temperature" of a color has no physical basis, but blue greens and blue violets, which seem to recede, are called "cool" colors; and reds, red oranges, and red violets, which seem to advance, are called "warm" colors.

Effects of Types of Light

Since color may be thought of as reflected light, it should be recognized that the kind of light that falls upon an object will affect the object's apparent color. A color that appears to be bluish green when viewed in daylight will look yellowish green in incandescent light. Under daylight fluorescent lighting—which does not contain all the colors of the spectrum—the same color will appear to be completely blue. As the reader will see in Chapter 3, colors must be selected in the same kind of light as that in which they are to be used.

Effects of Surroundings on Colors

There are certain other phenomena which should be kept in mind when selecting colors for an interior space. There must be, for instance, a delicate balance between the several colors used: one color must predominate. A wall painted in a bright color will seem to be larger than it actually is, because a bright color is more stimulating to the retina than a grayed hue. A white area surrounded by a darker area appears to swell in dimension. If the same color is used in several parts of an architectural space, it may appear to be different in hue in different places because of the variation in the amount of light to which it is exposed and also because of the proximity of the other colors. An area painted yellow will seem larger than one painted orange, and an orange area will seem larger than one painted red. Invariably, a blue area will seem larger than a black one. A bright yellow pillow will not look the same on a cool gray sofa as it will on a tan one. The fabric of a chair will seem to change if it is moved from one background color to another. In short, colors affect one another. Used by itself, a color will often seem adequate in a given location, but when used near

[1] R. W. Burnham, R. M. Hanes, and C. J. Bartelson: *Color: A Guide to Basic Facts and Concepts,* New York: John Wiley & Sons, Inc., 1963, p. 2.

another color—even one of the same color family—it will suddenly appear to be "dirty." A yellowish green, for instance, can make certain shades of blue look purple when they are used together. A very dark shade of, say, mulberry used on a wainscot will make a very pale shade of the same color used on the upper wall appear white.

The fact that colors look different in different surroundings has led to many disappointments when colors have been selected for decoration with no thought of their eventual neighboring colors. Many a beautiful vase has been purchased because it looked magnificent in a carefully prepared store display, only to become just another item when placed in incompatible surroundings in the home. This phenomenon is also responsible for the fact that women are frequently disappointed in dresses they have bought: in the store the dresses were displayed under ideal conditions.

In interior design, colors of deep value, such as deep violet (in the chromatic circle Plate III), will seem to be heavier than pale colors, such as yellow. These deep colors can cause an imbalance in a room if too much of the deep color is used on one side or in one area. Finally, it should be remembered that light colors, or tints, always look brighter if they are viewed against a dark background, while dark hues usually seem more dramatic against a white background.

If a room is painted with one of the cool colors, the apparent size of the room will be increased. If one of the warm colors is used, the room will seem to be smaller. Bright colors such as yellow oranges, yellows, and yellow greens have a luminous quality and should be used to lighten an otherwise dark room.

Chromatic Circles and Solids

As science developed, an increasing amount of attention was given to the secrets of color and their relation to mankind. Robert Boyle discovered in the seventeenth century that red, yellow, and blue come from white light by reflection and refraction. Sir Isaac Newton, while trying to solve the problems of the telescope in 1666, noticed the refraction and dispersion of light through a prism. He discovered that all color is contained in sunlight and that when a beam of light passes through a prism the direction of the light waves is changed (the violet waves, for example, are bent more sharply than red) and a rainbow results. Having obtained this information, Newton then formed the first chromatic circle by bending this sequence of colors, pulling the red and violet ends around, and joining the ends with purple. Johann Wolfgang von Goethe (1749–1832), the German poet, also dabbled in color and produced his own color wheel (Figure 2.2).

FIG. 2.2 Goethe's color wheel

COLOR SYSTEMS

There are in general use today several systems of color arrangement with which one can work according to his needs. These may be referred to as "object-color systems" in which color samples are organized according to colorant characteristics, according to color stimulus synthesis, or according to color responses. The uses of the systems vary depending upon the basic plan of organization.[2]

One general plan for constructing systems of object-color standards is called the Colorant-Mixture Plan, since it is based on the systematic mixture of pigments or dyes. In this plan, a limited number of dyes or pigments is used to develop the object-color

[2] *Ibid.,* p. 159.

gamut through the mixture of these materials in systematically varied proportions. One of the more complete colorant-mixture systems available is the Martin Senour Nu-Hue Custom Color System.[3] This system was developed from eight basic paints: six chromatic, one near black, and one white. The Nu-Hue system contains 1,500 colors, and is available either in a set of 3- by 5-inch cards in a plastic case or in the Colorobot, a portfolio of more than 1,200 colors arranged in a series of ten double-page spreads. The system covers the "color solid," an orderly arrangement of colors roughly spherical in shape, in almost equidistant steppings of hue, value, and chroma. The Colorobot is displayed in horizontal slices across the color solid at twelve value levels. Each level shows the complete hue and chroma range for that value level.

For each of the colors in the Nu-Hue system, the amounts of each of several of the eight base paints are known, and it is possible, by carefully mixing the various paints according to formula, to produce a satisfactory match for any of the colors shown. The Nu-Hue system includes paints usually used for houses, both exterior and interior. As the base paints were chosen for permanence, there is some restriction in the range from red purple to blue. Similar systems have been developed by other paint manufacturers, such as the Colorizer system, the Pratt & Lambert Calibrated Colors system, and Devoe Paint Company's Library of Colors, to name a few. The Plochere color system is also a colorant-mixture system.

A second general plan for constructing systems of object-color standards is called the Stimulus Synthesis Plan. One of the more complete color stimulus systems used in American industry is the *Color Harmony Manual*. This was taken from the German Ostwald system and developed from thirty object colors of different dominant wavelengths and maximum obtainable purity.[4]

The colors are arranged in a hue circle which consists of 24 colored chips (in this case made of painted cellulose acetate). The circle starts with yellow as 1, red as 7, blue as 13, and green as 19. All the colors have been so located that the opposite number of each hue is its complement. However, to further complete color description, intermediate colors have been included, two each, at yellow (24-1/2 and 1-1/2), red (6-1/2 and 7-1/2), and blue (12-1/2 and 13-1/2) to give a complete circuit of thirty colors.

A third general plan for constructing systems of object-color standards is called the Appearance Plan, in which color intervals are judged according to scales. The intervals between hues in an appearance system are determined by trained observers who judge the size of the intervals.[5] The Munsell color system, which falls into this category, was developed from judgments based on hue, value (brightness), and chroma.

The Munsell System of Color

One of the best-known and widely used systems of color standardization used in the United States today is that developed by Albert H. Munsell. He became greatly interested in the practical application of color, and was disturbed by the fact that the popular names for colors do not describe them adequately for professional purposes. They are named after flowers or plants, such as violet, indigo, old rose, primrose; after fruits, such as peach, pomegranate, grape, avocado, plum; after places, such as french

[3] *Ibid.,* p. 164.
[4] *Ibid.,* p. 165.
[5] *Ibid.,* p. 168.

Color Tree

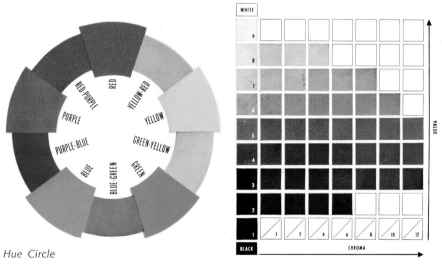

Hue Circle

Chart for 5PB

All-color Design & Marketing, Inc., New York, N.Y.

I. The Munsell Color System

Container Corp. of America, Chicago, Ill.

II. The Color Harmony Manual System

blue, naples yellow, or prussian blue; or after persons, such as Davy's gray or Hooker's green.[6]

Essentially the Munsell system consists of an orderly arrangement of colors in the shape of a three-dimensional color solid (see Plate I). It is based on a color circle of ten "major hues," made up of five "principal hues" (red, yellow, green, blue, and purple), and five "intermediate hues" (yellow red, green yellow, blue green, purple blue, and red purple). All of the ten major hues, which appear to be about equidistant to the spectator, are number 5 of a group of ten numbers. That portion of the outer circumference of each segment, such as red, red yellow, etc., is divided into ten segments and the whole hue circle is, therefore, composed of 100 hues. The center segment of each color is the true color such as red, red yellow, yellow, and the remaining segments in each hue section vary in color according to their proximity to adjoining colors. For instance, red, as it gets closer to yellow, contains more yellow. A scale of reflectances or "values," as they are known in the Munsell system, extends like a core through the center of the hue circle. A supposedly perfect white (one having 100 percent reflectance) is located at the apex of the value scale and is numbered 10. At the bottom, a supposedly perfect black (0 percent reflectance) is numbered 0. Nine graduated value steps connect these poles.

Radiating from this scale of values, or central core, are the increments of saturation (called "chroma" in the Munsell system). These, too, seem to be about equidistant to the spectator. The numbers of these increments vary from 0 at neutral gray to as high as 16, according to the amount of saturation produced by a given hue at a given value level. Since colors vary in chroma, or saturation, some colors extend farther from the neutral axis than others, and the solid is, therefore, not symmetrical. Pure red, with a chroma of 14, for instance, extends farther than blue green, with a chroma of only 6.

Munsell notation: Through an intricate system of notation, each hue is described by a letter, which locates it on the 100-step equator; a number from 1 to 9, to give its value; and another number to locate it in relation to the neutral axis.

With this information it is possible to describe exactly any given hue and to locate its place in the color solid. Furthermore, as Munsell stated,[7] one can "select one familiar color, and study what others will combine with it to please the eye," by the use of three typical paths: one vertical, with rapid change of value; another lateral, with rapid change of hue; and a third, inward, through the neutral center, to seek out the opposite color field. All other paths are combined by two or three of these typical directions in the color solid.

In addition to providing an excellent picture of color relationships in these dimensions, the Munsell "color tree" provides a splendid methodical way of standardizing, categorizing, and identifying colors. *The Munsell Book of Color*, which provides "an orderly array of color reference samples representing Munsell 3-dimensional color space," now provides the method accepted by the American Standards Association[8] for the identification of color. It is widely used by industrial and business firms.

The Ostwald Color System

While on the one hand the various parts of the Munsell system are made up of *hue*, *value*, and *chroma*, the Ostwald system, also in use, concerns itself with *hue*, *black*,

[6] As Munsell has said: "Can we imagine musical tones called lark, canary, crow, cat, dog, or mouse, because they bear some distant resemblance to the cries of those animals?"

[7] A. H. Munsell, *A Color Notation*, 2nd ed., Boston: George H. Ellis Co., 1907, p. 10.

[8] Now the United States of America Standards Institute.

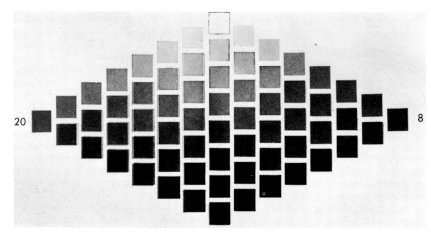

FIG. 2.3 The Ostwald Color Solid

FIG. 2.4 Vertical section through the Ostwald
Color Solid

and *white*. The Ostwald solid (Figure 2.3) is in the form of a double cone rather than a sphere. In this system there are twenty-four hues around the equator, and eight value steps from white at the top, or north pole, to black at the bottom, or south pole.

If the solid were to be cut in half vertically, the resulting section would be diamond shaped, as in Figure 2.4. Each side (left and right) of the diamond would form a triangle. All the colors in the left one would, for instance, be derived from Hue 20 (green) and those in the right triangle from Hue 8 (red). Hues 20 and 8 are complements, since they appear opposite each other on the hue circle. The entire solid is, of course, made up of twelve sections such as this.

Since each section is made up of fifty-six colors, the complete solid contains 672 chromatic colors, plus the eight steps of the gray scale. In each color triangle, those vertical scales parallel to black and white (the isochromes) are equal in purity. Those colors parallel to a line between pure color and white (the isotones) in the top portion of the cone contain an equal amount of black. Those scales parallel to a line between pure color and black (the isotints in the bottom) have equal white content. It may be seen from this description that the Ostwald system is based upon the assumption that all colors may be mixed from combinations of pure hue, white, and black.

Ostwald notation: Combinations of various numbers and letters make up the Ostwald color notations (see Figure 2.5). The hues, all full colors (free of white and black) numbered from 1 to 24, are arranged in groups of three. These groups are respectively called yellow, orange, red, purple, blue, turquoise, sea green, and leaf green (Figure 2.5). The gray scale (see Figure 2.7) is lettered from A for white at the top to P for black at the bottom. Two of these letters are always required (see Figure 2.6): the first indicates that the color contains the same amount of white as the gray of the gray scale in which the series ends. The second letter indicates that the color contains the same amount of black as the gray of the gray scale in which the series ends. In other words, any two *letters* will specify the amount of white and black of a color in terms of the gray scale. Any *number* from 1 to 24 specifies hue, and is written at the beginning of the notation like this: 22 PA.

Like the Munsell color tree, the Ostwald color solid may be used for the selection of color harmonies. These are located according to geometric relationships within the

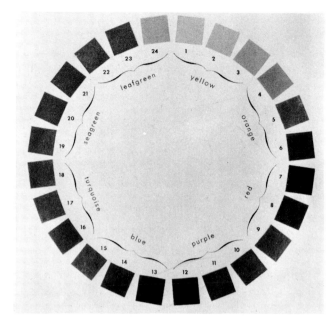

FIG. 2.5 Hues around the equator of the Ostwald Color Solid

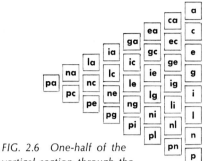

FIG. 2.6 One-half of the vertical section through the Ostwald Color Solid, showing the color notation

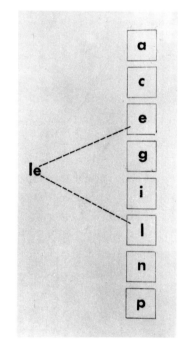

FIG. 2.7 The gray scale of the Ostwald Color Solid

various parts of the solid itself.[9] This more or less mathematical system is best understood when one examines the *Color Harmony Manual,* which was based upon the Ostwald system.

The Color Harmony Manual

Published by the Container Corporation of America, this system contains a hue circle of thirty colors and a nine-step gray scale. It also contains a total of 943 individual removable chips, matte finish on one side and glossy finish on the other, formerly sold mounted on a plastic tree (Plate II). These chips are now mounted systematically on heavy loose-leaf pages in a carrying case. This system is used by many artists, architects, and interior designers, and it is widely employed in industry for color control and color matching. A "Descriptive Color Names Dictionary," supplied as a supplement to the third edition of the *Color Harmony Manual,* lists "the best known American color names" for the colors in the manual. In addition, there is a series of diagrams of each of the various hues of the manual, and names descriptive of the colors are printed in each position (see Figure 2.8). The preparation of the dictionary was done by experts, and frequent reference is made to other well-known works on color names. Work is now being done to determine corresponding Munsell notations for both sides of each chip in the *Color Harmony Manual* (see page 30). According to the "Manual of Operation" of the *Color Harmony Manual* (page 17): "The Color Harmony Manual serves best as a tool in the hands of a colorist. It is not intended to limit or condition any use of color in any design treatment. . . . However, the internal order of the collection suggests relationships which the colorist may wish to consider and apply in accordance with his own interpretation."

[9] Egbert Jacobson, *Basic Color: An Interpretation of the Ostwald Color System,* Chicago: Paul Theobold & Company, 1948, Part II, pp. 56–108.

In the discussion of two- and three-color harmonies, the manual further states (page 28): "The choice of hue cannot be determined by rules, for it is fundamentally a matter of suitability. However, assuming adequate contrast (interval) in hue and lightness and darkness, the following general relationships will in most cases lead to useful and often unexpected harmonies":

1. "Any two colors of the same hue will go well together."
   Example: Hue 6 ia—Brite Coral Rose
   Hue 6 ic—Coral Rose

2. "Any two colors with the same two letters go well together."
   Example: Hue 6 ea—Brite Shell Pink (or Coral Pink or Pastel Pink)
   Hue 8 ea—Rose Pink

3. "Any color goes well with the two grays which have its letters."
   Example: Hue 15 le—Medium Blue
   e on gray scale or l on gray scale

4. "Any two colors with the same first letter go well together."
   Example: Hue 3 pg—Golden Brown
   Hue 15 pg—Dark Cerulean Blue

5. "Any two colors with the first letter of one the same as the second letter of the other go well together."
   Example: Hue 4 nc—Russet Orange
   Hue 7 pn—Dark Rose Brown

6. "Any two colors with the same second letter go well together."
   Example: Hue 1 pg—Dusty Olive
   Hue 14 lg—Cadet Blue (or Shadow Blue)

7. "Any two colors will go well with a third, the notation of which is any regular combination of their letters."
   Example: Hue 1 pg—Dusty Olive
   Hue 14 lg—Cadet Blue (or Shadow Blue)
   Hue 7 1/2 lg—Rose Mauve

8. "Any lc) may be combined with any (ic
   Any ig)   (lg
                                      (gc
                                      (li"

   Example: Hue 7 1/2 lc—Strawberry
   Hue 14 ic—Copen Blue or Sky Blue
       or
   Hue 14 lg—Cadet Blue or Shadow Blue
       or
   Hue 14 gc—Pastel Blue or Wedgwood Blue
       or
   Hue 14 li—Dark Gray Blue or Dark Steel Blue

   Hue 14 ig—Fog Blue (or Medium Gray Blue, Slate Blue, Steel
       Blue)
   Hue 1 1/2 ic—Light Antique Gold
       or
   Hue 4 lg—Light Spice Brown (or Sandalwood or Toast Tan)
       or
   Hue 6 1/2 gc—Dusty Coral
       or
   Hue 14 li—Dark Gray Blue

9. "Any ni) may be combined with any (nc
    ec)   (ie
                                        (ic
                                      (ne"

Example: Hue 19 ni—Dark Teal Green
             Hue 5 nc combined with Burnt Orange (or Persimmon)
                    or
             Hue 21 ie—Jade Green
                    or
             Hue 2 ic—Honey Gold (or Light Gold)
                    or
             Hue 6 ne—Redwood

             Hue 6 ec—Powder Rose
               combined with
             Hue 6 nc—Light Lacquer Red (or Coral Red)
                    or
             Hue 9 ie—Rose Plum
                    or
             Hue 5 ic—Light Persimmon
                    or
             Hue 11 ne—Deep Purple Mulberry

10. "Any na) may be combined with any (ng
    pg)   (pa
                                      (ga
                                    (pn"

Example: Hue 1 1/2 na—Brite Yellow (or Goldenrod, or Dandelion)
               combined with
             Hue 2 ng—Dull Gold
                    or
             Hue 6 pa—Brite Coral Red (or Vermilion)
                    or
             Hue 12 1/2 ga—Brite Periwinkle Blue
                    or
             Hue 9 pn—Dark Eggplant

             Hue 9 pg—Raspberry Wine (or Red Plum)
               combined with
             Hue 11 ng—Dark Purple
                    or
             Hue 11 pa—Purple
                    or
             Hue 12 1/2 ga—Brite Periwinkle Blue
                    or
             Hue 1 pn—Dark Olive

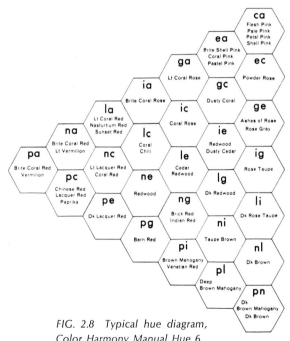

FIG. 2.8 *Typical hue diagram,
Color Harmony Manual Hue 6
Container Corp. of America*

Many other points in connection with the use of the *Color Harmony Manual* are covered in its "Manual of Operation." These points include the selecting of multicolor harmonies with—theoretically—as many as thirty-five colors which will harmonize with a given color. Of course, the architect or interior designer usually uses no more than two or three colors in varying shades in any given color scheme. To use more is to complicate a scheme and invite disaster.

Other Object-Color Systems

Some color systems in use today combine characteristics of the three general plans, hereinbefore described. These systems include the Maerz and Paul *Dictionary of Color* and the *Villalobos Colour Atlas*. Specialized color systems have been developed to grade items such as printing inks, soils, fruits, flowers, vegetables, etc.

Dictionary of Color Names

It is interesting to note that various groups of color investigators have adopted different color names: biologists use one set of terms, horticulturists another, and manufacturers of molded urea plastics and polystyrene plastics still another. Geologists do not use the color names for their rock-color charts that postage-stamp collectors use for their stamps. The architect and interior designer are probably most affected by Federal Specification TT-C-595 for Ready-mixed Paints and the color cards of the Textile Color Card Association of the United States, which use different names to describe their colors. The latter association issues two sets of colors each year: those which are in general and continuing popular use, and those which change according to season and style.

There is available for reference *A Dictionary of Color Names* compiled by the Inter-Society Color Council and the National Bureau of Standards (ISCC–NBS). This dictionary records about 7,500 color names, all annotated so that it is possible to translate one color vocabulary into another and relate color names to the Munsell system. It is possible, by means of an intricate system of organization and notation, to use the dictionary in many different ways. Under the heading "Beige" (page 88) we find three listings, plus over a dozen beiges with modifiers such as beige-light, beige-mode, beige-rose, beige-yellow, etc. Further study discloses the following:

Beige in Maerz and Paul, *Dictionary of Color*, 1st ed.
is described as "Pale Yellow–Grayish Yellow"

Beige in Taylor, Knoche, and Granville, *Descriptive Color Names Dictionary*
is described as "Light Grayish Yellowish Brown to Light Olive Brown"

Beige in *Textile Color Card Association, Standard Color Card of America
and U.S. Army Color Card*
is described as "Light Grayish Brown"

From this starting point, it is possible to find the Munsell designation for the color, or to locate a similar color in one of the other color systems, such as Plochere. Under the general category of *89—Pale Yellow,* we find that Maerz and Paul list thirty-two shades, Plochere thirty-eight, Ridgway eight, Taylor, Knoche, Granville nine, Textile Color Card Association two, and other sources twenty-three.

The dictionary is National Bureau of Standards Circular 553, 1955, and is available from the U.S. Government Printing Office, Washington, D.C.

The Difference between Light and Pigment

Unfortunately, the same laws do not apply to colors in light and colors in pigment. Physicists generally believe that red, green, and blue violet are the three primary colors. It is impossible, however, to obtain a full-intensity yellow with such a pigment mixture. Therefore, the chromatic circle that uses red, yellow, and blue as its primaries, while not agreeing with the physicists, is the most satisfactory for use by architects and interior designers. While a large variety of colors can be obtained by mixing pigments of these three primaries, a different set of primaries is needed to produce the widest possible range of pigment colors: magenta red, yellow, and blue green (cyan). These are the primaries of printing rules. A knowledge of the qualities of the pigments themselves and of the way they mix is important to the person who supervises the mixing of paint. With this knowledge he can produce any hue required.

The person who wishes to select and develop color schemes will find that, in addition to the Munsell and Ostwald systems, the simple chromatic circle shown in Plate III is of great assistance in determining color schemes and harmony. The chromatic circle can be used to study color relationships and to locate color harmonies. To begin with, it is a constant reminder of the relationships of pure colors one to another. For instance, red, yellow, and blue are called "primary colors" and are located at the third points of the chromatic circle, with yellow at the top. Green, violet, and orange are termed "secondary colors" and are located halfway between two of the primary colors. "Tertiary colors," situated between the primary and secondary colors, are yellow green, blue green, blue violet, red violet, red orange, and yellow orange. It is a basic arrangement, each element of which can always be found in the same position. It provides simple color categories into which all pigment names must fall. In addition, it provides a tool which one can use in imagining the same colors with a change of value (brightness) and intensity, in the three-dimensional manner such as that employed in the Munsell and Ostwald systems.

The work of the architect and the interior designer, by and large, is done with products which are the end results of the research and manufacturing techniques of others. While there are instances when the architect or interior designer will be called upon to specify and help to develop special colors and designs, he usually deals with finished products. His ability must lie in combining them so that the end result will have the desired effect. The very diversity of the colors available to the architect and the interior designer in these finished products aids him in creating effective and artistically satisfying architectural spaces.

When one is composing a color scheme for any given project, it is not as important to know the exact Munsell or Ostwald notation for a fabric color as it is to know that the fabric will be appropriate for its use, will look well in the type of light that is to be used, and will take its proper place with other colors that may subsequently be selected for paints, flooring, and furniture. In short, the architect or interior designer requires a simple system which permits the use of colors in appropriate relationships and flexible enough to use the many available products.

The Chromatic Circle and Its Use

The rules for pigment color harmony, like the rules for the study of color in light, are based on preferences, or taste, of most people. The guidelines set down here will be found to relate closely to the rules that nature seems to use in her colors. We seldom see colors used in full intensity in the world around us, and where intense hues occur, they are usually in small amounts (Plate XXI). Nature's spring and summer greens are not harsh, but are soft, grayed, yellow greens; browns in fall and winter are soft red, green, and yellow browns. The sky usually has very pale hues. Since the average person is attuned to the natural world about him, he can accept such subtleties more readily than the (usually man-made) harshness of loud, clashing colors.

It should be recognized at the outset that good color schemes employ only a few colors, properly selected, mixed, and blended. The difference between good art and "calendar" art can be largely explained by this restraint. The professional interior designer uses many shades of just a few colors, while the amateur is inclined to use a great many more colors than he needs for the job at hand. By doing so, the amateur provides himself with more problems than he can handle and introduces so many conflicting notes that his work becomes unpleasant to behold.

The color schemes listed below are guideposts only, but guideposts which can be used with ease. After you have learned the rules, you can stretch and bend them, constantly analyzing the results of your variations and adding the findings to your store of professional skill and judgment. You may then not consciously think of the rules when you are designing in color, any more than a professional golfer thinks of rules when he plays in a tournament. The rules of color may be modified—or completely disregarded, as they sometimes are by the great painters. New color concepts may be formulated. But first, try the rules below; the results will surprise you.

One or Two Colors with Black, White, or Gray   The simplest of all schemes is that in which one or two colors are used with black, white, or gray. The average book cover (without the dust jacket) is an example of this kind of scheme. An executive office might have walls covered with off-white grasscloth with a black pattern, two club chairs in medium-blue leather and two side chairs black fabric with the carpet dark blue.

The Monochromatic Scheme   The monochromatic color scheme, simple but attractive, is one in which many shades of a single color are used. Of course, not all colors will lend themselves to a monochromatic scheme simply because the lighter colors cannot achieve deep enough values for emphasis. This limitation automatically eliminates yellow, orange, and pale green. A living room might be executed in a monochromatic scheme using walls of pale blue green with a wainscot of medium blue green. The carpet might be deep blue green. The sofa could be medium blue green, wing chairs a deep blue green, and side chairs a pale blue green.

The Analogous Scheme   The analogous color scheme permits the use of colors which adjoin each other on the chromatic circle (Plate III), such as yellow, yellow green, and green, or red, red orange, and orange. These colors are not necessarily used in their pure form in various parts of the scheme, but are mixed together in varying amounts so that numerous shades may be developed from the few colors used. It is usual for one of the colors in such a scheme to predominate, that is, to be used in greater amounts than the rest. A bedroom might be developed as follows: Walls medium-deep yellow orange (copper); carpet pale gold (yellow); bedspread deep yellow orange (copper); wall hanging white, pale yellow, and medium orange; chairs pale yellow and white.

Analogous Scheme plus Complementary Accent   A common type of color scheme consists of a series of analogous colors plus a complementary accent, i.e., a color on the opposite side of the chromatic circle from the center of the analogous run. For example, a scheme that uses yellow orange, orange, and yellow green could be combined with violet. By mixing these colors together in various amounts it will be found that the complementary accent (violet) will gray and soften the three analogous colors, deepen them for the darker tones, and at the same time complement them. This scheme might be used in a small cafeteria. The end wall could have a mural of a Japanese scene in black and white with yellow-orange accents. The sofas against the wall might be black; the chair seats might be yellow orange and white, orange and white, red orange and white, or turquoise and white (complementary accent).

Complementary Scheme   For a simple complementary scheme, two colors opposite each other on the chromatic circle, such as blue violet and yellow orange, are
used. Neither of these need be used in pure form; literally hundreds of shades may be
obtained by blending them together in varying amounts. An interesting aspect of complements is the way the colors affect each other. In pure form they actually complement each other; each has the quality of making the other look better by its proximity.
But as they are mixed together (as in paint or dye), they modify each other to the
point where they finally form a neutral gray. It should be noted, however, that the
neutral gray obtained by mixing different sets of complements will vary; sometimes
a mousy gray occurs, and at other times a warm, brownish gray .

Grays can be formed in paint or dye by mixing any two complements, such as red
and green, yellow and violet, orange and blue, or red orange and blue green. A tie
score is as unsatisfactory in color as in a ball game, and since completely neutral
grays seem to have no color at all, they are to be avoided or used sparingly. It is wise
to use more of one complement than the other so that the resultant mixture clearly
contains more of one color than the other. The same principle holds true in the
selection of fabrics. Bright yellow, for instance, might answer your needs in a color
scheme; but it is quite possible that a grayed yellow, made with a mixture of blue
violet and yellow, would look better.

Another interesting phenomenon is that colors appearing in neither pigment sometimes appear when two complements are mixed. With certain proportions of yellow
and blue violet, a rust color will appear. A little experimentation will illustrate this
point. Using tempera, which mixes like most of today's interior house paints, mix
the various complementary colors together in pans and watch what happens to each
hue as it is blended in varying amounts with its complement.

A complementary scheme in a dining room might use blue green and red orange.
One wall could be hung with a scenic wallpaper containing white, blue green, and
some red orange, while the other three walls could be painted pale blue green.
A carpet of taupe (a mixture of blue green, red orange, and white) and curtains of
red orange and blue green on white would complete the scheme.

Near, or Split, Complements   A split complement takes the form of a Y on the
color wheel, the one arm of the Y pointing, for instance, to yellow orange, the other
arm to yellow green, and the stem of the Y pointing to violet. A split-complement
color scheme, then, is composed of a color plus one color from each side of the
direct complement of the first color. This resembles the complementary scheme, but
provides a slightly wider range of colors and shades.

For example, red, yellow orange, and blue green might be employed in an executive's office as follows: Three walls papered in a pattern of blue-green and yellow-
orange leaves and branches on a warm gray background, and the fourth wall covered
with a blue-green grasscloth. The carpet would be beige, the executive's chair deep
brown-red leather, and the side chairs medium blue-green leather.

Double Split Complements   A double split complement takes the form of an X
on the chromatic circle with, for example, the top legs pointing to yellow orange and
yellow green, and the bottom legs pointing to red violet and blue violet. These colors,
used in a young girl's bedroom, might be distributed as follows: White walls, curtains
of a print containing varied amounts of all four colors on a white ground, a bedspread
of yellow green, chairs with white frames covered in blue violet, and the floor
has a gray carpet, whose color is obtained by mixing red, violet, and yellow green.

Triads   Another excellent color scheme may be obtained by the mixture of triads, that is, three colors located at the third points of the chromatic circle. For instance, red, yellow, and blue might be used in a traditional living room by having the walls and carpet off-white, the curtains a print of medium blue and pink on an off-white background, a sofa upholstered in damask containing grayed yellow and medium blue, and a wing chair and side chairs covered in a medium-blue fabric. The triad combination provides a wide range of hues, shades, and tints.

A fact to be kept in mind regarding all color schemes excepting the monochromatic is that different kinds of colors and mixtures thereof may be obtained by varying the pigments that are used. In other words, the three different sets of orange and blue complements can be obtained by using three different kinds of blue on your palette, such as cobalt, french ultramarine, or cerulean. A red and green complementary color scheme permits the use of either Hooker's green or emerald green. A yellow violet complementary color scheme can be carried out with either cadmium yellow pale or yellow ochre.

Browns are a mixture of orange with blue, green, or gray; grays result from mixtures of three primary or two complementary colors. The type of gray—warm or cool—can be mixed to suit. It must be remembered that the colors represented in a scheme may or may not appear in the pure form. In a triadic color scheme, for instance, beige walls may be a mixture of yellow ochre, cobalt blue, alizarin crimson, and white. A wood color in the same room may contain the same colors, but in different proportions. A chair may be a shade of cobalt blue, a sofa of yellow ochre, a pillow of pure red, etc.

Ready-mix Paints

There are on the market many premixed paints produced by the several paint manufacturers. The number of hues available varies according to the make: the smaller the company, generally speaking, the smaller the number; the larger the company, the larger the number. Books of paint chips may be seen in any paint store, and these will vary in size from a thin pamphlet to a book or books containing 1,500 colors or more (see page 24). Some of these books are arranged according to color categories, with all the yellows, yellow oranges, oranges, red oranges, reds, red violets, violets, blue violets, blues, blue greens, and yellow greens presented in sets, each color in each set being labeled by number as well as name. Some companies use names only; some use numbers only. The names seemingly are selected not only for their descriptive quality, but also for poetic memory appeal. Some typical color names (not interrelated) are listed below:

Pratt and Lambert	Benjamin Moore	Eastern Paint & Varnish Co.	Glidden
Antique Gold	Empire Gold	Absinthe	Smoke Rose
Apple Blossom	Honey Beige	Alice Blue	Spray Blue
Autumn Haze	Antique Pearl	Bamboo	Parakeet
Ballerina Pink	Apricot	Blue Dawn	South Sea
Blue Smoke	Flame	Blush	Fiesta
Cornflower	Willow Green	Citron	Flamingo
Copper Glow	Crystal Blue	Conch Shell	Coral Reef
Evening Cloud	Spring Green	Dove	Cotton Candy
Flamingo	Pink Ice	Enchantment	Old Cedar
Gypsy Red		Green Banana	Sea Flower
Horizon Blue		Innocence	Straw
Inland Sea		Jonquil	Chive
Jade		Mulberry	Blue Ridge
Pink Champagne		Queen Anne's Lace	Lucerne

The foregoing can be compared with the names designated in the Inter-Society Color Council–National Bureau of Standards *List of Standard Hue Names and Abbreviations* adopted in 1939:

Name	Abbreviation	Name	Abbreviation
Red	R	Purple	P
Reddish orange	rO	Reddish purple	rP
Orange	O	Purplish red	pR
Orange yellow	OY	Purplish pink	pPk
Yellow	Y	Pink	Pk
Greenish yellow	gY	Yellowish pink	yPk
Yellow green	YG	Brownish pink	brPk
Yellowish green	yG	Brownish orange	brO
Green	G	Reddish brown	rBr
Bluish green	bG	Brown	Br
Greenish blue	gB	Yellowish brown	yBr
Blue	B	Olive brown	OlBr
Purplish blue	pB	Olive	Ol
Violet	V	Olive green	OlG

Now while the names of some commercially produced colors bear a marked similarity even though they are manufactured by different companies, the colors themselves are usually dissimilar. One company's "beige" will be deeper than another's; still another firm will label a tan brown "beige." As a matter of fact, no two colors in the author's collection are exactly the same. This is because each paint manufacturer wants his colors to be unique. Furthermore, it sometimes happens that various batches of ready-mix paint will vary as much as a couple of shades. These differences are caused by variations in raw materials. The color chip may be a soft gray blue, but the paint purchased may be a brighter or deeper blue. Sometimes the difference is so slight that only a trained eye can detect it, but often the difference is great. Such paint can sometimes be corrected with tinting color, but just as often it cannot. This difficulty is particularly trying when fabric and paint are to match, and the fabric has already been purchased and installed.

How, then, can one obtain exactly the paint color that the job demands? One can use white plus Universal Tinting Colors, but even these will vary with the manufacturer. If the author had his choice, his tinting colors would be similar to those used in tempera painting, and might include the following:

Yellow (spectrum)	Light blue
Dark yellow	Blue (spectrum)
Yellow ochre	Ultramarine blue
Orange (spectrum)	Emerald green
Vermilion	Green (spectrum)
Red (spectrum)	plus
Dark red	White and Black

(Spectrum colors are those which are primary or secondary colors on the chromatic circle.) With these, practically any color can be mixed. However, each manufacturer sells a slightly different set of tinting colors. The three listed below are much like others:

Pratt & Lambert	Benjamin Moore	Merkin
Hansa yellow	Hansa yellow	
Chrome yellow light		Chrome yellow light
Chrome yellow medium	Chrome yellow medium	Chrome yellow medium
Chrome yellow deep	Chrome yellow orange	Chrome yellow orange
Yellow ochre		
Raw sienna	Raw sienna	
American vermilion*	Chinese vermilion	Chinese vermilion
Venetian red	Venetian red	Venetian red
English rose lake*		Crimson red
Ultramarine blue*		
Palco blue	Thalo blue	Thalo blue
Green dark		
Green medium	Chrome Thalo green medium	Chrome Thalo green medium
Palco green	Thalo green deep	
Green light	Chrome Thalo green light	Chrome Thalo green light
Burnt sienna	Burnt sienna	Burnt sienna
Raw umber	Raw umber	Raw umber
Burnt umber	Burnt umber	Burnt umber
Drop black		
Lampblack	Tinting black	Tinting black

* Recommended for tinting interior paints only.

All of the above colors are deep in tone and, of course, can be lightened by adding white. When lightening a color, however, remember that since white contains a great deal of blue, it not only lightens but also changes some colors. For example, vermilion when lightened with white turns to vermilion pink, and chrome yellow orange turns to orange pink.

It is important, too, to remember that yellow ochre and raw sienna, while they look somewhat alike, are different and affect other colors differently. It should also be remembered that while most colors are readily identifiable by name, the earth colors are not, and should be memorized. When lightened, raw sienna is gray yellow, burnt sienna is gray pink, burnt umber is pinkish brown, and raw umber is a warm neutral gray. Black, when lightened, becomes bluish gray.

Finally, it must be said that the tinting colors listed above will not give you every color you want. There will be times when you will have to buy tubes of artists' oil colors to get the proper results. There is absolutely no blue like cobalt blue, no red equal to alizarin crimson, and no yellow similar to yellow ochre for the mixing of certain colors.

But compare the splendid list of colors available today with, for instance, the few colors that were available to the architects of colonial Virginia. Some of these were: Fig blue, lampblack, spanish brown, prussian blue, yellow ochre, white, and red. But while the paucity of colors limited the architect, a great variety of hues resulted from the mixing of the several pigments.

THE DEVELOPMENT OF THE COLOR PLAN

The creation of a color plan for any architectural space requires the application of established guidelines for creative reasoning, including:

1. Exploration of the field in which the problem arises.
2. Formation of a hypothesis (the solution of the color problem).
3. Development of the hypothesis to discover its implications.
4. Progressive testing and verification of the hypothesis by repeated observation.

In solving a color problem, one would determine the following:

1. The proposed use of the space.
2. The size of the space.
3. The orientation of the space.
4. The type of person or persons who are to occupy the space.
5. The length of time the space will be occupied by various people and their activities during that time.
6. The existing colors surrounding the space under consideration.
7. The client's (or clients') preferences regarding color and style. If these are incompatible with your findings, ways must be found to modify the client's thinking in order to preserve the integrity of the color plan.

When the analysis of the problem has been completed, the following decisions must be made:

2. Preliminary Findings

1. Determine the color plan that is to be used:
   a. One or two colors with black, white, or gray
   b. Monochromatic
   c. Analogous
   d. Analogous with complementary accent
   e. Complementary
   f. Split complement
   g. Double split complement
   h. Triad
   i. Other

The color plan must, of course, include the colors you desire for walls, floor, ceiling, furniture, and furnishings. For example, if you intend to use yellow on the walls, it is obvious that yellow must be part of the color scheme selected.

2. Determine the colors that will be used in each part of the room and decide on their intensities. Color balance must be developed by carefully selecting areas and volumes that are to be light, dark, pale, or intense in color.
3. Evaluate the scheme for appropriateness.
4. Evaluate the colors in relation to each other to make sure that they are compatible.
5. Evaluate the colors and color scheme in the natural light of the space as well as the artificial light that will be used.
6. Make adjustments required by these findings and continue to refine and improve the color plan.

3. Development

The development of the color scheme will include the actual selection of materials:

1. Examine your collection of ready-mix paint colors to determine whether stock paints can be used. If the colors must be mixed on the job, it is well to experiment

with these paint colors and tinting colors first so that you can intelligently direct the painter at the job.

2. Research the market for wood, wall coverings, furniture, fabrics, carpets, and other materials in the colors you require.

3. Evaluate your findings and modify, adjust, or change your color plan as necessary.

4. Experiment with variations of your final color plan to introduce individuality.

4. Presentation to Client

1. When you are commissioned to work on a project, it is wise to ask your client to withhold all decisions or purchases with regard to color until you have had time to complete your study.

2. The presentation of a color plan to a client should be complete, clear, concise, and accurate. There should be no opportunity for misunderstandings.

3. Reevaluate all facets of the problem at this time. You can still change or modify items, if you so wish, before work is begun.

5. Execution of the Project

1. Be sure to communicate carefully and accurately with all persons involved in the ordering of all items. Order by company name, number, and color.

2. When deliveries of items are made, check again for accuracy.

chapter three

THE EFFECT
OF LIGHT ON COLOR

IN the field of interior color, the expression "true color" has no meaning because
light is such a variable item. There are times when a room will be lighted by daylight only and times when artificial light will be used. At other times both daylight
and artificial light will be present. By true color do we mean the color in daylight? If
so, do we mean the color by daylight in the morning, at midday, or in the late after-
noon? Do we mean true color on a hazy day or on a bright, sunny day? Do we mean
the daylight of New York, Miami Beach, or Athens? All of these are quite different,
because of the difference in clarity of the air and other factors. A color which is popular in one part of the world probably obtained its popularity because it looked good
in that particular location. In the past certain colors were widely used because they
looked good in candlelight. The same colors look totally different under different kinds
of artificial light.

We know, then, that light modifies colors in an almost infinite number of ways.
How can we apply this information to the use of color in interiors? First, let us be
sure that we realize that the colors we select or mix should be seen in the light in
which they are to "live." The fabric on a chair may look good in a department store
or showroom, but used in different light in the home it may not be as attractive. A
nubby fabric, well lighted, will have one color; in a dimmer light, it will have a
duller color. Lighting arrangements must be carefully considered: Will colors be subject to spot lighting, reflected light, or diffused lighting? Will colored bulbs or colored
filters be used? The skillful architect or interior designer will take all these factors into
consideration when colors are being selected. Frequently he will make adjustments
in the lighting or the color scheme as the job progresses.

Daylight

The colors that will be selected in, say, a house will be determined in part by their location: will they receive daylight from the north, east, south, or west? Generally speaking, one should use warm colors on the north, cool colors on the south, and neutral colors on the east and west. However, these colors are usually modified by other factors, such as the light reflected from other buildings and trees, the function of the room, and the prime hours of use of the room.

Incandescent Light

We must determine whether the artificial lighting is to be incandescent, fluorescent, mercury-vapor, or a blend of these. Incandescent has a relatively large red component. There was a time when incandescent fixtures were the only type available; they are still the most common type. The average person, therefore, is accustomed to thinking of incandescent light as the norm. Incandescent lamps are available in a variety of sizes, shapes, and types. Clear lamps should be used only when diffusing materials are employed so that the bulbs are hidden from direct view; diffusing materials or shielding reflectors are often built into the fixtures themselves. Inside-frosted lamps diffuse the light, eliminate striation, and help suffuse shadows.

A number of colored lamps are made by The General Electric Company and other lamp manufacturers. These provide special lighting effects for shops, hotels, restaurants, and special displays. The lamps are made in various colors, including Dawn Pink, Sky Blue, Spring Green, and Sun Gold. The light from each color is softened by the ceramic enamel coating on the lamp bulbs, and the bulbs accentuate the red component of color. This warm component is present in all four of the above colors; they can be used with any color scheme since they enhance the appearance of skin tones as well as paints and other interior finishes. Colored bulbs for ceiling installations are also available as floodlights in pink, blue white, yellow and amber, and other tints. When a number of colors are used together, the resultant light resembles a soft white light. (Plate IV, Dining Room: "Equal numbers of pink, blue white, and yellow reflector bulbs mixed together make a general effect that is somewhat like white light, but far more stimulating.")

For built-in lighting, where tube-shaped incandescent bulbs are desired (in niches, coves, displays, and luminous panels), or wherever a continuous line of incandescent light is desired, lamps such as the General Electric Lumiline may be used. These are made in white, clear, and frosted finishes, as well as in a number of colors, including Moonlight Blue, Emerald, Orange, Surprise Pink, Straw, White, and Red.

Fluorescent Light

When fluorescent lighting was first used, it was hoped that it would approximate daylight in color—it was quite blue and quite lacking in the warm tones. People soon discovered, however, that "daylight" fluorescent changed colors violently: food frequently appeared to be spoiled and inedible, people looked pale and unattractive, and the color of makeup and clothing changed. Over the years, however, other fluorescent lamps were put on the market. Today the following are available:

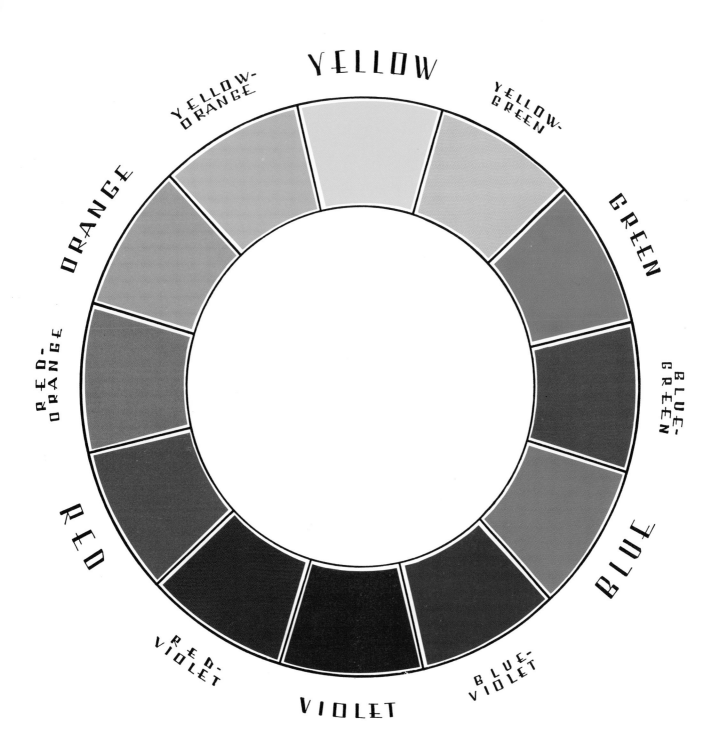

III.   Twelve-hue Chromatic Circle

General Electric Co., Cleveland, Ohio.

IV. Dining Room. Equal numbers of pink, blue-white, and yellow reflector bulbs mixed together to produce an effect that is somewhat like white light but more interesting.

Daylight (D)   Deluxe Cool White (CWX)
White (W)   Warm White (WW)
Soft White (SW)   Deluxe Warm White (WWX)
Cool White (CW)

The first three are the older versions of "white," and they are still used. But the last four (known as the simplified line) are generally used today for most purposes.

From the above list it may be noted that fluorescent lamps are now designated partially by color. The lamps designated warm emphasize yellow, orange, red, and red purple. The cool lamps emphasize blue purple, blue, blue green, and yellow green.

The General Electric Company has recently introduced a mercury lamp which has approximately the same effect as Cool White fluorescent.

Both the lighting level and the color of the light affect the appearance of colored surfaces. Filament lamps and warm fluorescent lamps, being deficient in blue, emphasize red. Thus they accent warm hues and "gray" cool hues. The Warm White and Deluxe Warm White fluorescent tubes are similar to the filament lamp.

Of the lamps which supply cool hues, the Cool White Deluxe is more nearly like that of daylight than Cool White. Although Cool White and Warm White lamps do not render color as well as Cool White Deluxe and Warm White Deluxe, they are generally thought to be a most efficient source where black-and-white–seeing tasks are to be illuminated. (See charts, page 42.)

Following is a list of lamp colors recommended by The General Electric Company for various tasks and locations:

Art studios, art classes, etc. ....CWX
Apparel shops—sports or daytime wear ....CWX
    Evening wear ....WWX
Barber and beauty shops ....WWX
Bowling alleys ....CW
Color inspection and grading ....CWX
Classrooms ....CW
Delicatessens ....CWX
Drugstores ....CWX
Florists ....CWX
General office areas ....CW
General work areas—no critical color work ....CW
Hardware stores ....CWX
Homes and apartments ....WWX
Hotel, motel guest rooms ....WWX
"Intimate" areas—lounges, restaurants, areas of residential character, etc. ....WWX
Jewelry stores ....CWX
Private offices ....CWX or WWX
Shoe stores ....WWX
Supermarkets, groceries, meat markets ....CWX
Variety stores ....CWX

Structural Lighting

Structural, or built-in, lighting may include such lighting as that behind curtain valances, wall brackets, cornices, coves, luminous wall panels, and diffusers, above luminous ceiling panels or floating canopies, under soffits, and in niches and coffers. While it is not the purpose of this book to go into the design of these various installations, there are a number of points that must be remembered when structural lighting

Color Effects of White Fluorescent Lamps

	Cool* White	Deluxe* Cool White	Warm† White	Deluxe† Warm White	Daylight	White	Soft White— Natural
Lamp appearance; effect on neutral surfaces	White	White	Yellowish white	Yellowish white	Bluish white	Pale yellowish white	Pinkish white
Effect on "atmosphere"	Neutral to moderately cool	Neutral to moderately cool	Warm	Warm	Very cool	Moderately warm	Warm, pinkish
Colors strengthened	Orange, yellow, blue	All nearly equal	Orange, yellow	Red, orange, yellow, green	Green, blue	Orange, yellow	Red, orange
Colors grayed	Red	None appreciably	Red, green, blue	Blue	Red, orange	Red, green, blue	Green, blue
Remarks	Blends with natural daylight	Best overall color rendition; simulates natural daylight	Blends with incandescent light	Excellent color rendition; simulates incandescent light	Usually replaceable with CW	Usually replaceable with CW or WW	Usually replaceable with CWX or WWX

Color Effects of Mercury and Filament Lamps

	Mercury	White Mercury	Color-Improved Mercury	Deluxe White Mercury	Filament
Lamp appearance; effect on neutral surfaces	Greenish blue white	Greenish white	Yellowish white	White	Yellowish white
Effect on "atmosphere"	Very cool, greenish	Moderately cool, greenish	Warm, yellowish	Moderately cool	Warm
Colors strengthened	Yellow, green, blue	Yellow, green, blue	Yellow, green	Orange, yellow, blue	Red, orange, yellow
Colors grayed	Red, orange	Red, orange	Blue	Green	Blue
Remarks	Poor overall color rendering		Color rendering often acceptable, but not equal to any white fluorescent	Color rendering good; compares favorably with CWX fluorescent	Excellent color rendering

* Greater preference at higher levels.
† Greater preference at lower levels.
Source: General Electric Co.

is used. For instance, in residential work, especially, Deluxe Warm White fluorescent lamps should be installed. The recesses of the several different types of installations should be painted flat white, and the lamps used in each element of built-in lighting should be from the same carton, since even a slight variation will be very obvious. All lamps should be of the same color and tube diameter, and both the channels and the lamp holders should be white. It should be remembered that light which strikes a wall obliquely gives the wall a glowing quality. It is soft and uniform, but since the top of the furniture is lighted and reflects this light, one must be wary of cracked, rough walls. A rough plaster ceiling may appear to be soiled. Drapery materials used with such grazing light should have light backgrounds, and their patterns must be chosen with care. Designs of small figures are desirable, since the effect of the pattern will be accentuated.

The various kinds of built-in lighting are most effective when dimmers are used. These provide additional flexibility in the lighting design and mood.

Portable Lamps

Portable lamps enable one to adjust lighting to individual needs. The color and design of all the lamps in a room should relate to each other and to the furniture. Lamp shades of certain colors—red in particular—should be used sparingly, since they tend to distort light. A colored shade should be lined with white unless an unusual effect is required. Generally speaking, a lamp should provide light for easy seeing. The primary light source is at the bottom of the lamp, but some light should come through the shade, and some should reflect from the ceiling. The height of the lamp should be adjusted according to the use: decorative, reading, working, etc. (see also Chapter 7 page 119).

Reflectance

A surface, whether of paint or some other material, absorbs some light and reflects the rest. The amount of light that is reflected in proportion to the total amount falling on it equals the reflectance value of a color.

If one is designing the lighting for an existing installation, the amount of reflectance provided by the interior finishes must be taken into consideration when the required amount of light is being computed. In a new installation, the lumen method of lighting design requires that you know the reflectance of the colors of your interior finishes. A number of paint companies give the reflectances for each of their colors; you can judge the reflectance values of the colors you intend to use by comparing your colors with those whose reflectance values are known. Reflectance-value charts used by architects and designers are also helpful. A number of shades of each color are shown, together with the reflectance of each. Reflectances of various kinds of wood are also sometimes given. The reflectance of any color chip or wood sample can be determined by comparing it with reflectances on such a chart (Plate V). Needless to say, the colors that are used on any given job will be determined by reflectance value *as well as* other factors such as suitability, individual taste, comfort, and the general aura or desired impression required of the job. A general guideline for reflectances is as follows:

Reflectance Range for Interior Surfaces

Ceilings:	60 to 85 percent (white or pale tint)*	
Walls:	35 to 60 percent†	
Window or	Fabric treatment:	
Glass Wall:	Wide expanse or backgrounds	45 to 85 percent
	Limited areas of decorative design on light background or side draperies	15 to 45 percent
Floors:	15 to 35 percent (25 to 35 percent preferred)‡	
	(Values at high end of range recommended for use in rooms where lighting efficiency is a major consideration: kitchen, bathrooms, utility rooms)	

* 70 percent or more is required for effective performance of indirect lighting methods.

† Appreciably higher than 50 percent creates brightness problems when portable luminaires are placed near walls and when extensive wall lighting methods are used. According to paint manufacturers, the public prefers 45 percent.

‡ Middle to high values preferred because of their predominance within the 60-degree cone of vision when performing many visual activities.

Source: Illuminating Engineering Society, *IES Lighting Handbook*, 3rd ed., New York: 1959, p. 15–3.

Munsell value scales for judging reflectances are also available. The reflectances of these scales were scientifically determined by direct measurement and by mathematical analysis.

It is interesting to note that when a gray surface and one of another color are exposed to the same amount of direct light, they will be equally bright. However, if the same two surfaces are exposed to light that has been reflected several times, as in indirect lighting, the gray surface will have a lower reflectance value than the other. Much consideration must be given to this aspect of light and color.

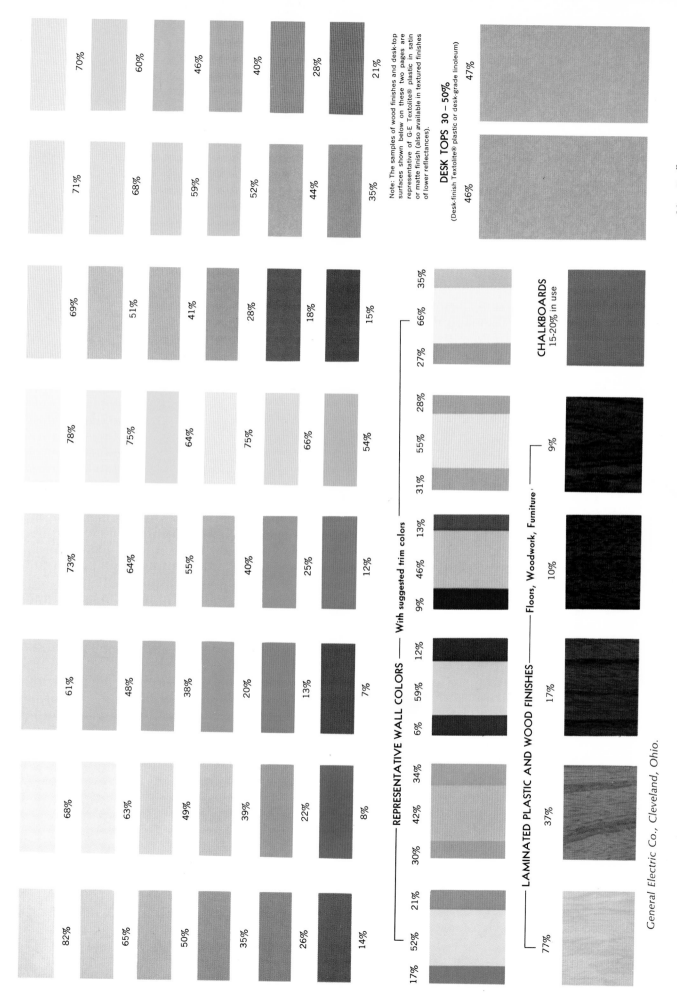

V. Reflectance-value Chart

70% 60% 46% 40% 28% 21%

71% 68% 59% 52% 44% 35%

Note: The samples of wood finishes and desk-top surfaces shown below on these two pages are representative of G-E Textolite® plastic in satin or matte finish (also available in textured finishes of lower reflectances).

DESK TOPS 30 – 50%
(Desk-finish Textolite® plastic or desk-grade linoleum)

47%

46%

69% 51% 41% 28% 18% 15%

78% 75% 64% 75% 66% 54%

73% 64% 55% 40% 25% 12%

61% 48% 38% 20% 13% 7%

68% 63% 49% 39% 22% 8%

82% 65% 50% 35% 26% 14%

35% 66% 27%

28% 55% 31%

13% 46% 9%

12% 59% 6%

34% 42% 30%

21% 52% 17%

REPRESENTATIVE WALL COLORS — With suggested trim colors

CHALKBOARDS
15-20% in use

9%

10%

17%

37%

77%

LAMINATED PLASTIC AND WOOD FINISHES — Floors, Woodwork, Furniture

General Electric Co., Cleveland, Ohio.

Zebrawood

English brown oak

Teak

Kevazingo

Brazilian rosewood

William L. Marshall, Ltd., New York, N.Y.

VI. Samples of Unfinished Wood

chapter four

THE
PSYCHOLOGICAL
EFFECTS OF COLOR

GENERAL

B Y observation, one may see that various colors have a strongly emotional effect on most people. It has been known for some time, for instance, that blue reduces excitability and therefore helps one to concentrate. Blue is both cooling and sedative, but it cannot be used indiscriminately, because too much of it may produce melancholia. These qualities of blue were discovered during the Middle Ages, and are partially responsible for the use of so much blue in the stained-glass windows of the great Gothic cathedrals.

Green seems to be cooling, and it acts as a sedative. Yellow, as one may note from sunlight, is cheery, stimulating, and attention-drawing. It is the most luminous color. On dull days, when the yellow of the sun is absent, most people exhibit mental and physical sluggishness and a general lack of enthusiasm for their work; when the sun appears again they become more active. Yellow also demands attention, and so it is used in dangerous locations, such as the edge of a subway platform, to mark the hazard.

Red is exciting and stimulates the brain. Medium red suggests health and vitality; bright red often has amorous connotations. Red also has an aggressive quality and is frequently associated with violence and excitement.

Purple, sedative and soothing, was originally made from the Purpura shellfish of the Mediterranean. The dye from this shellfish, which was used for royal robes in ancient times, was so expensive that only the wealthy could afford it.

Orange has a stimulating effect and should usually be used in relatively small amounts. The occupant of an orange office, for instance, will become ill at ease after a short time and will leave it at every opportunity. Brown is restful and warming but should be combined with orange, yellow, or gold because it can be depressing if used alone. Gray suggests cold and, like brown, is depressing unless combined with at least one livelier color. White, on the other hand, is cheerful, particularly when used with red, yellow, and orange.

Generally speaking, most people prefer either warm or cool colors. Personal preference depends on such factors as the individual's familiarity with various colors and color schemes and the emotional connotations, conscious or unconscious, that they have for him. A psychological reaction against a color, say blue, may occur in a person who as a child was punished by being made to stay alone in a blue room. Similarly, a person will prefer colors that were present during pleasurable experiences. The color needs and desires of each individual must, therefore, depend on a great many factors, the important point being that color likes or dislikes must be discovered before a color scheme is determined for him. As Albers has said: ". . . we change, correct, or reverse our opinion about colors and this change of opinion may shift back and forth. Therefore, we try to recognize our preferences and aversions against what color dominates our work, what colors on the other hand are rejected, disliked, or of no appeal. Usually a special effort in using disliked colors ends with our falling in love with them."[1]

The great schools of painting have established characteristic color schemes, and those people who are fond of a particular period of painting will also usually be fond of the colors found in those paintings. The relatively low-keyed colors used by Rembrandt, for instance, are often found in the home of one who is fond of Rembrandt's work. Similarly, the brilliant colors used by most contemporary artists are frequently present in the homes of those who admire contemporary art. The choice would seem to be a personal one.

There are, of course, other reasons for individual sensitivity to color. They will vary from the color-blind person to the person who is hypersensitive to color. Color sensitivity varies even among those with normal color vision. It sometimes changes with age and with the physical condition of the individual. A person who can usually tolerate a color may find it intolerable when he does not feel well. A person may like a certain color in small amounts, yet dislike a large area of it.

It ought to be clear, then, that color should be used with care. An individual may use whatever colors he prefers in his own home, but he should not feel that he can use any colors he likes in a public or commercial building. He must strive for a color scheme that will be attractive to a majority of the thousands of people who will use the building.

Since most people prefer a sense of order, they prefer a color harmony which is based upon an orderly plan. For example, a color scheme made up of colors that have something in common will appeal to most people. If the color scheme of a room is to be made of yellow ochre, cobalt blue, alizarin crimson, and white, the wall color may be made by mixing all three colors and white so that a beige results. The furniture, carpet, and color accents of the same room may be shades of the same yellow, red, and blue, or they may be made by mixing any of these three colors together in varying quantities to provide a "color family." Colors that are similar, such as yellow

[1] Josef Albers, *Interaction of Color*, New Haven, Conn.: Yale University Press, 1963, p. 25.

and yellow orange or blue and blue green, will look good when used together, since they are related.

Generally speaking, young children prefer brilliant, bright colors, including the primaries, but as they grow older their tastes become more subtle.

A woman may like a logically determined residential color scheme that she selects this year; it may irritate her next year when she reads in a popular magazine that her color scheme is no longer "in" because it does not use the new "colors of the year." On the other hand, the repainting of a famous old room will inevitably bring wrath down upon the head of the person who changes it if the new colors are not historically correct.

There is, in the United States, the phenomenon called planned obsolescence. An automobile bought this year will be out of style next year, simply because a new design exists. One must, therefore, purchase a new car each year or lose status in his neighborhood. The same rule holds true for clothing, household appliances, and the colors of one's house. Now, a properly planned color scheme will always be beautiful—but to the lady of the house the problems caused by planned obsolescence are very real, since she must keep up with the Joneses.

Demand is created by changing peoples' tastes, and if they read and see enough of what is "new" and "desirable" they find it almost impossible to resist. Common sense, however, should tell one that what was beautiful last year will always be beautiful unless it deteriorates physically.

Although a great deal of color is selected emotionally, and even irrationally, it must be remembered that guidelines exist which, if used, help to keep the color designer on the proper path. The architectural space and all things in it must be studied as a unit to achieve an appropriate, as well as beautiful, color scheme. Color fixations must be dealt with, whether they are fixations of the color designer or of the client. Certain shades of green and brown, which are normally tolerated by most healthy persons, may make someone who is not feeling well quite ill. A sufficient number of color changes normally exist in a residence to provide psychological contentment. But in large buildings it is often necessary to deliberately vary the colors in the different parts of the building so that most of the colors of the spectrum may be seen by the occupants during the workday. Color can be used functionally. It can be made to draw attention to (see Plate XXXII) or minimize the importance of a wall. It can be made to maximize or minimize the size of objects. It can be used to help express architectural forms—or it can, if carelessly used, destroy architectural form. One must remember that color on walls, floor, and ceiling is modified by other colors that are present in the same area. For instance, if three walls of a room are a warm gray and the fourth wall is a shade of yellow, the yellow will be reflected in the gray walls and will modify their appearance. Again, pale gray green may look good in a room until a bright shade of green is used next to it. Suddenly the gray green looks very gray and quite inadequate.

An enclosed room (i.e., one without an outside view) which is painted with warm colors makes those who work in it feel warm. Similarly, a large, open, windowed space with a great deal of glass, painted with cool colors, will sometimes make people who work in it feel chilly.

One is "prepared" for a room's color if the entrance is painted a complementary color. Deep colors always seem to make the walls of a room seem heavy, while pale pastel colors seem to make the walls light. If a room is long and narrow, its appearance can be modified by painting the end walls warm colors—yellow, red, orange. Similarly, in a small room, the walls can be made to recede by painting them with cool colors, such as green and blue. A long corridor with many doors can be visually shortened by painting the two side walls different colors, the end walls in cool colors, and the doors each a different color.

From the above it will be seen that color can be made to modify form and, therefore, must be used with great care and skill if it is to help and not hurt architecture. An excellent amalgamation of color and architectural form may be seen in Plate XX.

As we have noted in Chapter 1, color has been used in many different ways throughout history. Sometimes the palette has been quite limited (see Plate XXIX); at other times it has been diverse. The preference for color, even today, varies not only according to style, but also by geographical location. Greenish blue with yellow and gray or white is popular in Scandinavian countries. In France, the traditional French colors are used in contemporary color schemes. These include, for example, light green, light blue and rose of the Louis XV period, the delicate tints of green, blue, gray, and dusty pink of Louis XVI, the rich, strong persimmon, orange, and yellow of the Directoire, and the deep green, yellow, gold, coral, and black of the Empire period. Even in the United States, which draws its taste from many lands, color usage varies according to location. While it may be said that one may use any colors he wishes in his own home, one should use restraint in choosing colors for a public or a jointly owned building.

RESIDENTIAL

It must be recognized that residential colors must be tolerated by the whole family. If members of a family have tastes which differ widely, they may be satisfied by allowing them to select the colors of their own rooms.

Residential color schemes, particularly those which are arrived at without any professional help, usually reflect current "taste" as seen in magazines or furniture stores. If these colors bear no relation to the location in which they are to be used, catastrophe frequently results, and a color designer is often called to correct the situation.

When a color scheme is being designed, certain problems arise immediately: Shall the walls be pale or deep in color? What parts of the room are to be light, medium, or dark in value (for contrast)? Shall the color scheme be cool, or warm, or neutral? How sophisticated is the client? An interior space can be made beautiful in itself, but it will not necessarily complement the people who will use it. A skillful hand, however, can create a beautiful, restrained, and integrated colored space that will make its occupants look healthy and handsome.

A living room with a great deal of red in it will detract from the beauty of a woman's red dress! Couples should work together in selecting colors. The plan of living of a household group should be studied before any color selections are made. If the man of the house is engaged in a business which uses a great deal of his energy, he should have a retreat at home—a room with a quietly harmonious color scheme. If, on the other hand, his day is spent in a monotonous business, he probably will enjoy color contrasts and bright colors in his home.

As we have said before, most people prefer either warm or cool colors; this preference must be immediately determined. The next item that must be considered is personal color likes, dislikes—and fixations. The author has on a number of occasions worked with clients who would accept any color as long as it was shocking pink! Trying to dissuade such a client is like trying to take opium from an addict. Finally, old wives' tales about all shades of green being good for the eyes must be refuted, and the client persuaded to use a suitable shade of green.

Approximately half of the average clientele will like pastel shades and the other half deep colors. Sometimes those who prefer pastel colors have simply not had the courage to enjoy brilliant colors or vice versa, or the professional help they needed to choose well.

The architecture and orientation of a house or apartment will largely determine the colors that are to be used. A well-designed contemporary house may have colorful furnishings and accents (see Plate XIX). Walls or parts of walls are sometimes of natural-finished wood, stone, or marble. But architectural spaces which already exist do not always have such beautiful interior materials and in these cases, beauty must be obtained by applying paint, fabric, etc. upon walls and ceilings. Frequently an otherwise uninteresting dark space can be transformed by the use of sunny yellows, pinks, reds, tangerine, white or black, and warm lights. Bold colors stimulate conversation in a living room, but should not be used in bedrooms since their very brilliance may create insomnia. Often it is possible to bring deeper colors into such a space. The several shades of rust, blue, and yellow sometimes seen in stone outside one's room may be brought inside and used in a more brilliant fashion. While it is well to keep the major colors in a room low in key, walls, rugs, pictures, and furniture may be made brilliant with unusual colors such as lemon yellow, lime green, pink, and orange. The success of all colors used, will, of course, depend upon their use in the specified location, the amount of each color, the light that will fall upon it, and the relationship of colors in each room to each other and to the central scheme.

COMMERCIAL

The commercial institution is a home away from home for many people, and the inclination to introduce some of the principles used in residential work is always present. It must be remembered, however, that all the colors in such an installation must relate to each other and to a central scheme, and that a personal choice which conflicts with the appearance of the general scheme cannot be tolerated.

There are a number of reasons for such color control, the main one being that there is usually a certain amount of circulation of personnel; one sour note will stand out and become an object of ridicule. It must be remembered that members of a commercial organization must be willing to concede certain things for the good of all. Color likes and prejudices must not be permitted to enter the picture.

In most cases the walls of the lobby of a commercial building should be stimulating and exciting, and the corridors should be neutral so that when the doors of the offices are open harmony will be apparent. Individual offices may vary in color, texture, and materials, but they must have a basic similarity. The offices that will receive cold light, of course, should have warm colors, and vice versa; but within this framework certain small variations may exist. Even though orientation is taken into consideration in the selection of colors, each color must be tried during the design period in the exact location and in the kind of artificial light that will be used. If, in addition to general light, downlights and spotlights are to be used over pieces of sculpture, paintings or other wall decorations, these should be switched on so that their effect can be noted.

While it is not the purpose of this book to discuss in detail the works of art and accessories that are to be used in various offices, these items should be selected and positioned by the same person who designs the color schemes.

Although it is not possible to take into consideration the psychological needs of each worker in a large office, it is interesting to note that in cool-colored rooms some people will constantly complain about the cold or the air conditioning, while in rooms with warm colors some people will frequently complain that their air conditioning is not adequate. For this problem there seems to be no answer except to relocate the person.

Of course, the main objectives in determining the color scheme of a commercial installation is to provide colors which are rich, definite, and harmonious (see Plate XXVIII), which will be easy to live with, and which will contribute to the efficiency and well-being of all who tenant the building. Colors should be subtle; for example, no brash greens or blues should be used unless compensating colors are used with them. Where offices are located upon an uninteresting interior court, the colors of such offices should be sunny and brilliant.

If all the above suggestions are followed, and if the color designer is allowed free rein, the installation will usually be psychologically satisfying. If, however, each person in an organization is asked his opinion, the results will be completely disastrous since a successful color scheme cannot be designed by the consensus method.

INDUSTRIAL

As in the case of commercial installations, the kind of artificial light must be taken into consideration in the design of industrial interiors. It will depend, to a large extent, upon the type of operation performed. It goes without saying that a sufficient amount of light must be supplied. It is equally important that the proper *kind* of light be used to avoid shadows and glare. For ease of seeing, it is generally well to keep the wall color darker than the machines or work benches. If the space under consideration is large, the walls should be in the cool category (blues or greens). If the space is small, the walls can be warm in color (yellow, orange, etc.) However, if intense heat is produced by some of the processes in a space, the walls should be painted a cool color, regardless of the size of the space, to psychologically assist the workers to bear the heat. Similarly, in areas that are extremely cold, warm tones should be used on the walls.

Columns in nearly all industrial buildings should be brilliantly painted in yellow or vermilion to point them out to operators of trucks, fork lifts, etc.

Safety Color Guides

The United States of America Standards Institute, in cooperation with the National Safety Council, has promulgated a color code for marking physical hazards and certain types of equipment in industrial plants. The use of color in this connection provides quick identification of danger spots, even by persons who cannot read:

RED   Fire protection equipment and apparatus
      Danger
      Stop

ORANGE   Dangerous parts of moving machinery

YELLOW   Physical hazards that might cause stumbling, falling, etc.

GREEN   Safety—first-aid dispensary or kits, stretchers, safety deluge showers, etc.

BLUE   Caution against movement or use of equipment being worked on such as elevators,
      scaffolding, etc.

BLACK & WHITE   Traffic direction
                  Sanitation

In addition to the above, it is often necessary to identify pipelines in industrial installations. The following color code has gained widespread acceptance:

RED   Fire protection systems and equipment

ORANGE   Dangerous materials, nonflammable, such as acids, alkalis, toxic materials, gases,
      oxygen

YELLOW   Dangerous materials, flammable, such as fuel oil, gasoline, kerosene, alcohol, pro-
      pane, butane, acetylene, hydrogen, and solvent

GREEN   Safe materials, such as drinking water, service water, brine

BLUE   Protective materials

VIOLET   Valuable materials

BLACK   Electrical conduit

ALUMINUM   Steam[2]

EDUCATIONAL

It is important to know that although very young students prefer strong colors, as they grow older their taste becomes more sophisticated and subtle. Generally speaking, in contemporary schools, almost anything that can be colored is treated in a bright and brilliant way. Corridor walls, for instance, are sometimes yellow; rooms facing cool north light are given warm tones and those facing warm south light are given cool tones. The front wall of each classroom is often painted darker than the other walls of the room. Every effort should be made to select a color that will be approximately the same value as the color of the chalkboard, so as to minimize eye fatigue. While most colors in school buildings are pastel, bright accents are employed by painting columns bright blue, yellow, chinese red, or blue green. Doors and trim are darker than the walls in which they are located. Painted doors can be given variation and additional interest by making them various colors.

It goes without saying that there are sets of rules for using color in hospitals, department stores, retail shops, etc. Lack of space does not permit us to include this information here, but the reader will by careful observation be able to formulate guidelines similar to those given above. Each type of building has its own specified needs, however, and these must be analyzed before any color scheme is designed for a specific project.

[2] Pratt and Lambert, Inc., *Architectural Specification Manual*, 2d ed., p. 95.

VII. Varied Patterns of Veneer

Plain-sliced butternut

Quarter-sliced mahogany

Rotary birch

Half-round walnut

Comb-grain oak

Special Figures

Pencil stripe

Fiddleback

Mottled

Blistered

Stumpwood

Feather crotch

Crotch swirl

Birdseye

Crossfire

Ribbon stripe

Hardwood Plywood Manufacturers Association, Arlington, Va., and Fine Hardwoods Association, Chicago, Ill.

Colorado stone—Random Ashlar Pattern

Lava stone—Rubble Pattern

Pennsylvania mica—Sawed-bed Ashlar Pattern

Georgia crystal white marble—Sawed-bed Ashlar Pattern

Turquoise stone—Rubble Mosaic Pattern

Pine log—Rubble Mosaic Pattern

Bergen Bluestone Co., Inc., 464 Route 17, Paramus, N.J.

VIII.   Types of Stone

chapter five

THE
APPLICATION OF
COLOR: BUILT-IN
MATERIALS

W A L L hangings and wall coverings were first used to provide warmth in dwellings which were otherwise stark and cold. The members of the household, of course, produced the wall hangings, and since it took a long time to complete each one, they were few in number. In the machine age, it became possible to produce similar hangings and other interior finishes so cheaply that they could be owned by the masses. Today, ease of transportation and a worldwide market make such materials available to anyone who wishes to purchase them.

The arts-and-crafts movement has never entirely disappeared, but the cost of handmade items is prohibitive to many people. In addition, the supply is, of necessity, small. Frequently handicraft industries are developed because of abundance of skilled artisans in a given area, such as Nantucket, where magnificent fabrics are still produced on handlooms and marketed in the great centers of the world. Most people, however, have within reach a fabulous number of machine-made materials which are excellent in quality, inexpensive, and easily obtained and installed.

Now, it should be said at this point that because the education and taste of architects and interior designers differ, not all of them design in the same manner or believe in the same principles of design. Each of the four "schools" of architecture and interior design listed below has its own characteristic approach to color, but ideas, beliefs, and methods flow back and forth between them:

1. Organic architecture, with purity of treatment and use of materials, as practiced by Frank Lloyd Wright and his followers

2. The modern International Movement, as epitomized by the works of Le Corbusier, Walter Gropius, Miës van der Rohe, Marcel Breuer, and their followers

3. Historic purity

4. A combination of modern and historic

Frank Lloyd Wright, who believed that the outside and inside of a house should be "of each other," held that an "organic" building should seem to grow out of the ground, and that building and ground should be obviously related to each other. Similarly, he believed that the textures and patterns of draperies, rugs, and furnishings should be sympathetic in design and finish with the house in which they are placed. He believed that in organic architecture the materials should be used in their original state and should not be changed or modified in appearance by the application of paint, wallpaper, or other covering. He was unalterably opposed to the use of paint for covering wood; he felt that wood should be either unfinished or stained.

The designers of the International style within the modern movement strive for a synthesis of all demands and needs. They seek beauty in discipline, restraint, and the greatest possible refinement of all essential elements. They have broken completely with the past and have developed a new, dynamic style in which the volume of the interior of a building, as well as its exterior, is arranged so that its form and proportions create a coordinated whole. Asymmetry replaces symmetry. Simplification and a general lack of ornamentation, both inside and out, are important hallmarks of this style. Large wall areas, bare of ornamentation, and unbroken expanses of glass are used. Materials are carefully selected so that their beauty and natural qualities are expressed by skillful placement, proportion, and detail.

Generally speaking, furniture and furnishings are simple, functional, and an integral part of the total design. In many cases a building's furnishings are designed by the architect. At the beginning, such designs inspired an interest in architectural circles, and at the Bauhaus, from 1925 to 1928, a group of students began to experiment in the design of machine-made items such as tables, chairs, desks, and lighting fixtures. Many architects (like Marcel Breuer, who had taught at the Bauhaus) experimented later in the United States with the design of tubular metal furniture. Others, like Miës van der Rohe, began to design truly exquisite furniture such as his Barcelona chair (1929). Such were the beginnings of the design of modern furniture.

Designers of the third group use only historic forms and color, while the fourth group combines natural materials, manufactured materials, and modern architectural forms with eclectic patterns and forms. The colors used include pastel shades, medium hues, brilliant hues, and combinations of all three. Color and design are almost always asymmetrical. One or two walls in a room are often painted in deep colors, and the remaining walls or parts thereof constructed of a natural material such as wood or stone or painted gray or off-white. Accents are often brilliant in hue.

The selection of colors and materials varies with the group a designer finds himself in. A design produced according to the "less is more" philosophy of Miës van der Rohe will be completely restrained in the use of color, while an interior in, say, the fourth group listed may include an elaborate and unusual use of color. As for the client, he will often insist on a traditional interior in his home and a contemporary interior and color scheme for his office.

Interior finishes can, of course, be simple or elaborate, depending upon the budget, the desire of the client, the requirements of the job, and possibly, the length of time necessary for delivery. An architect may select a color for the brick in a building, only to find that it cannot be obtained in time. A shade of blue terra-cotta selected from a sample kit may be unavailable because it was discontinued the day before. But no matter what his beliefs or desires, the architect or interior designer has at his disposal many bread-and-butter colors which are usually available in brick, marble, and the newer materials. The latter, of course, are changed at least once a year. The colors and patterns of most products are selected because they appeal to most people, but many special colors originally developed for custom projects eventually become widely popular. Many of the synthetic materials achieve their initial popularity as inexpensive substitutes for expensive natural materials. With refinement, and the development of a good color line, these materials often attain a beauty and popularity of their own.

Regardless of what materials are used in any given design, success depends upon the proper relationship of parts as well as the correct selection of materials and colors for interior finishes. If one thinks of an architectural space as a work of art through which he can walk, he will realize that, even if the proportions of the room are correctly established and a sufficient amount of light is provided, correct materials, colors, and textures must be selected and strategically arranged so that the space is united and possesses harmony and balance. Color, materials, textures, and form must be brought together in such a way that they relate to each other without competing and are pleasant to be near. Just as the human being can be related to the height, width, and length of an architectural space by careful use of scale and proportion, so can he be related to the space by carefully locating just the right amount of each color used so that each part becomes a successful portion of a pleasing whole.

The art of creating such pleasing wholes is called interior design. Just as one has not mastered a language until he has gained a thorough knowledge of its grammar, so one must know available materials and their colors before he can be a successful designer. Much of the remainder of this book, therefore, is devoted to an overview of these materials.

WALL COVERINGS

Paint

There are two basic kinds of paint: true paint, which is a mixture of a pigment with a vehicle (the fluid component of the paint), and varnish, which contains no pigment. Generally speaking, each type of true paint may be obtained in various finishes, as follows:

Flat—used on most wall surfaces

Semigloss—sometimes used for trim

Eggshell enamel—used for trim

Ready-mix paints may be obtained in any paint store, and the colors available may be seen in color books or color charts. Very few paint stores handle all brands, and will inevitably have their favorites. Some paints are factory-mixed; others are mixed by a color-mixing machine in the paint store, according to factory-established formulas. It should be pointed out that although the color that you see on any given color chip should, theoretically, exactly match the color you get, there is always the possibility that the color of the paint will vary from that of the color chip. Even the smallest deviation from a formula originally determined by precise laboratory methods can produce a difference visible to the professional eye. To minimize the possibility of color variation, Martin Senour (which uses a three-dimensional color system based on hue, value, and chroma) advises that each color be mixed by an electronically controlled machine which matches the formula fed into it on a punchcard. Factory-mixed paints, while generally true in color, may occasionally vary from the sample chip and from lot to lot. This variation is caused, among other things, by variations in the pigments used.

The colors that are shown in manufacturers' color books are selected in different ways. Some are actual color increments based on the Munsell system, some are based on the Ostwald system, and still others are derived from specially developed systems. The various parts of the Munsell system are made up of hue, value, and chroma; the Ostwald system concerns differences in hue, black, and white. It is obvious, therefore, that the appearance of colors will vary according to the system used. Some colors will be clear and straightforward, while others will be softened and earthy. No matter what colors are used, it must be kept in mind that a color seen on a small chip will inevitably look much darker when it is on a wall. It should also be kept in mind that the same paint will look different on different walls because of the variations in intensity and quality of light in the various parts of the room.

A sample of any color must be tried in place before its true appearance can be ascertained. Most people find it difficult to carry a color in their minds; i.e., the average person simply cannot remember a color. Therefore, when searching for a matching color it is well to have a sample of the material you are matching. Remember, though, that you will never find a paint color that exactly matches a piece of fabric because the textures of the two will differ. A close match will be sufficient.

The range of available ready-mix colors is suggested by the lines of a few paint companies. Pratt & Lambert has 937 ready-mix colors in its Calibrated Colors system, Martin Senour has approximately 1,200 in its Nu-Hue color system, Colorizer has 1,322 colors, and Devoe Paint has some 900. Even with the thousands of ready-mix colors that are available, there may be times when one cannot find the correct shade for a particular project. It is true that most interior designers mix colors on the job, but this is because the color lines of, for instance, carpets and fabrics are not color-integrated. Although a pumpkin-colored paint may match the fabric being used, it may be too dark or too light for the carpet. It therefore becomes necessary to mix a batch of paint at the job for the exact shade required.

In order to supervise the painter in the mixing of special colors, the architect or interior designer must know how to mix colors himself. Not only must he know the basic principles of color theory (see Chapter 2), but he must also be able to analyze visually any color that he is trying to produce so that he will know what tinting colors should be used to obtain the desired results. Ideally, the novice should experiment with the mixing of colors by using white paint and tinting colors such as those described in Chapter 2. If this is impractical, it is possible to obtain similar results using tempera colors, as they react in a way almost identical to alkyd paints. Tempera will dry more quickly than oil, but experimentation using small wash dishes will save a great deal of time and money and give the novice good practice in the art of mixing paint.

Paint samples should always be made by first introducing a small amount of white paint in a white wash dish, then introducing small amounts of color. (If you begin by introducing colors in a wash dish, and then add white, you will soon have more paint than you require.) The same procedure should be followed when mixing paint for a job: i.e., start with white and carefully add tinting color. As mentioned in Chapter 2, the addition of white to a color does not automatically produce a lighter shade; sometimes the color becomes chalky and unrelated to the original color. In the same way, the addition of black to a color does not automatically darken the color, because black contains a great deal of blue and it often changes the color. Many interesting phenomena may be observed by mixing various colors together. Black and yellow make green, for example, and black and certain types of green make a soft shade of blue! Mixing colors is an enjoyable and rewarding process. It is wise to use small quantities of paint for the initial paint samples so that experimentation does not spoil large amounts of paint.

Small white index cards should be kept handy for trying out the colors and allowing them to dry. Sometimes changes will occur in the drying process, and you may want to compensate for these. Another word of caution: in mixing paints on a job, you will find that painters use different brands of white. These will vary from a gray white to a pink, yellowish, or bluish white. Obviously, if a color is not to have any pink in it, white containing pink should not be used. If it is not to have any blue, white without blue should be used.

Wallpaper

Wallpapers were originally a substitute for wall painting and decorative hangings. Their first use seems to have been in China, in small rectangular pieces, and they were introduced to France and England during the seventeenth century. The French worked up a domestic substitute with marble graining and small hand-painted or stenciled patterns. Flocks were imitation brocades and velvets. In the middle of the seventeenth century, Jean Papillon, a Frenchman, carved patterns in wood blocks and used them to produce printed wallpapers. These were the forerunners of wallpaper as we know it today. Later, printed panels replaced hand-painted wall designs. As styles of decoration changed, wallpaper designs were produced to harmonize with these fashions. Scenic papers were printed from about 1800 to 1850 and were very popular in Europe and America. About 1840, machine-printed papers on cheap backgrounds appeared.

Modern wallpapers are available in roller-printed (Figure 5.1a) and hand-blocked designs (Figure 5.1b) and scenic patterns (Plate X-A). Because more brilliant accents and subtler shadows are possible in the hand-blocked process, these papers are more beautiful than the machine-printed ones, but they are also more expensive. In addition, the repeat of a hand-blocked paper can be greater than that of a roller-printed paper, since the repeat in the latter is determined by the circumference of the roller. Scenic wallpapers are made in a series of vertical strips, that, when hung, form a mural-like wall decoration. Some modern designs are versatile. The designer can arrange the pattern as he wishes. For example, strips numbered 1, 2, 3, and 4 need not

FIG. 5.1   Wallpaper   (a) Roller printed

(b) Hand blocked

be used in numerical order, but may be used in any order desired; the parts may also be used on various walls of the same room.

Wallpapers vary in color and pattern from traditional to modern, from realistic to abstract. The grounds upon which wallpapers are printed are available in many colors and shades—white, gold, and silver, green, black, blue, amber, yellow, ivory, purple, pink, red, peach, and brown. Patterns are printed in colors which constitute carefully studied color schemes. For instance, a pattern of white and gold may be printed upon a wedgwood blue; or tangerine and brown may be printed on white. Each pattern is usually available in several choices of colors. For instance, one design might be available in the following combinations of colors:

1. Pink, orange, and green on a white background
2. Blue and green on natural grasscloth
3. Blue, green, and yellow on bronze silk

Another pattern might come in the following variations:

1. Brick, persimmon, and yellow green on a white ground
2. Violet, fuchsia, and gold on a white ground
3. Blue and lime on a white ground
4. Curry, orange, and brown on a white ground

If it is difficult to visualize how a color will look in a room, it is doubly difficult to visualize how a colored wallpaper will appear; much study is necessary to develop a knowledge of the effects of different patterns and colors. As large a sample as possible of the wallpaper should be obtained for the preliminary analysis of color, pattern, and scale. A large room will require a pattern containing large elements, and a small room calls for a pattern with small elements. The pattern and color of a wallpaper gives a feeling of movement that must be taken into account in the furnishing of the room. Usually a patterned wallpaper will cause a room to appear "busy," and so quietly-covered furniture should be used as a complement. A "busy" room also calls for less furniture than a room with walls of solid color. Frequently a single wall is papered and the remaining walls are painted.

A wallpaper can be obtained for every conceivable room, but what is appropriate in one place may not look good in another. While an entrance foyer may have an overscaled orange-tree pattern to delight the visitor, a bedroom should properly have a relatively soft and quiet paper. A dining area which is relatively small can be given greater depth by the use of a scenic-pattern paper on one wall to give a sense of perspective. The selection of wallpaper should be made with great care to ensure the most effective solution. Today's wallpaper designs vary from geometric to floral, from spot patterns to allover patterns. Modern usage calls for strong, clear colors in abstract patterns. A rose in a modern design, instead of being carefully and realistically delineated, is a splash of color with an irregular outline. Round spots become splashy, irregular shapes in an attempt to relate them to abstract or impressionistic art.

Wallpapers can be treated to make them washable. Sometimes this treatment is included in the manufacturing process; sometimes it must be added when it is purchased. Most wallpaper is sold in rolls containing 36 square feet, but packed in single (36 square feet), double (72 square feet), or triple (108 square feet) roll quantities. In figuring the amount of wallpaper required for a project, it is wise to check the exact size of the paper and the repeat of the pattern before ordering. To ensure a smooth surface, lining paper, a thin, low-cost paper, should be hung before the top paper is applied. It is always best to remove the old paper before applying the new.

FIG. 5.2 *Grasscloth*

(a) *Cellulose horizontal—*
stripe weave

(b) *Cellulose herringbone weave*

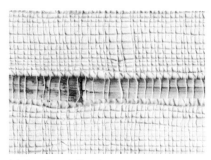

(c) *Reed and fine hemp—*
horizontal stripe

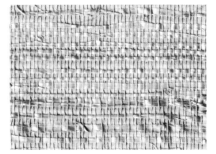

(d) *Grasscloth*

Grasscloth, long handcrafted in Japan, was first used on the walls of Buddhist temples. Since it is, for the most part, cottage-industry manufactured, it varies in color and texture, roll by roll and lot by lot. But these very variations contribute to its beauty and charm. The "grass" for the basic types of grasscloth is made of fiber taken from the inside of the honeysuckle vine. The raw material is soaked, cleaned, cut to strands of approximately the same width, dyed, woven on hand looms in various patterns, and mounted on thin paper. Although the usual undyed grasscloth varies in color from a brownish beige to a greenish tan, nearly 200 other colors and textures are available. Variations are obtained by including in the weave bamboo, threads, and papers of various colors, such as white, brown, green, yellow, taupe, black, gold, orange, and blue. The fibers of some grasscloth papers are dyed before weaving; these fibers are available in various reds, blues, and greens, and in a relatively muted yellow. Further variations are obtained by employing different types of weaves. The simplest is a basket weave; the more complicated range from linen-type weaves to highly sophisticated chevron patterns (Figure 5.2a to d). In addition, patterns are created by using two or more colors in rectangles, or by combining grasses of several colors and weaving them together with various combinations of regular and irregular stitching. In some designs, bamboo strips of varying widths are woven together in a continuous pattern; in others, they are woven together with grass which has been dyed a contrasting color.

The variety in grasscloth is almost endless. The striped patterns, however, are made to be used horizontally; it is almost impossible to align the pattern of one roll with that of the next. This limitation must be kept in mind. The variations in color and pattern contribute to the beauty and uniqueness of the overall effect, but it must be remembered that there will be unevenness in the continuity of the pattern.

For those who prefer them, there are grasscloths which contain silk, rayon, net, cellulose, and metallic papers, as well as various kinds of reeds. The silks are commonly known as *shikii* silks and are available in exotic iridescent shades.

Grasscloth requires care in application, but it provides no difficulty for the experienced paperhanger. It is available in the usual double roll which contains about 72 square feet, but there are variations in width according to texture and material, so the dimensions should be verified for each pattern.

Vinyl

Wallpapers can be given some measure of protection against soiling by the manufacturer or the consumer, but this protection is not always sufficient. In areas where walls will become quite soiled, because of heavy traffic or for other reasons, a heavy-duty covering is required. There is available on the market today a range of vinyl-coated wall coverings, some paper-backed, others cloth-backed, that is widely used. Vinyl plastic is also available for upholstery, but this section will deal exclusively with vinyl wall covering.

The patterns available in vinyl wall covering have, generally speaking, been inspired by wallpapers, grasscloth, and various fabrics, including silk, linen, and *bouclé*. The designers have also imitated wood, marble, stone, cork, leather, stippled rough plaster, and textured metals (see Figure 5.3a–c). Due to economic factors, no doubt, some patterns are available in only five colors while others are available in as many as thirty. In many lines, certain of the colors are common to several patterns. But for the most part the color line of each pattern ranges from pure white through pale tones (such as peach, pink, green, blue, and yellow) and medium tones to the darker shades of blue, green, brown, red, gray, and yellow. This variation makes vinyl wall coverings a versatile tool for the architect and interior designer.

Vinyl wall coverings vary in weight as well as in color and pattern. The weight should be determined by the use. Most manufacturers provide weight-usage recommendations. The success of a vinyl installation depends upon the skill of the installer, who should be expert in this work. Vinyl must be applied with a special adhesive which is usually sold by the manufacturer who supplies the vinyl.

Over the years, certain vinyls have proved to be more colorfast than others. Those in which the color is an integral part of the vinyl seem to keep their color better, but improvements in this field are being made constantly.

Printed patterns are available in vinyl in both stock and custom designs and colors. These are surface prints, however, and the designer must be aware of the fact that some cleansing processes may remove the pattern in a short time. Actual tests, using the exact methods of cleansing that will be employed after the vinyl is installed, should be repeatedly made on samples to determine their durability.

Vinyl wall coverings come in different weights and thicknesses. The weight of one brand varies from 22.5 to 36.0 ounces per linear yard in the 54-inch width. The thickness varies from 0.021 to 0.035 inches. Weight and thickness alone, however, do not determine how much abrasion a vinyl wall covering will stand. The density and purity of the vinyl mix is also crucial. One of the best-known abrasion tests is the Taber test, and manufacturers' literature should be checked for performance in this test.

Since vinyl wall coverings are frequently installed where fire protection is important, proposed patterns should be examined before they are purchased to make certain that they meet the requirements of local fire codes and authorities. The National Board of Fire Underwriters tests the flame-spread characteristics, smoke density, and toxicity of vinyl coverings, and manufacturers can supply the test results. It is important that these tests be accepted by all agencies having jurisdiction for use in buildings of various types. In extreme instances, it may be necessary to have special tests made.

FIG. 5.3 Vinyl wall covering

(a) Leather pattern

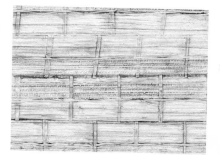

(b) Grasscloth pattern

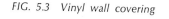

(c) Grass pattern

Wood

Of all the materials available to the designer of interiors, wood offers the greatest number of possibilities. It can be worked easily, it can be obtained in an almost limitless number of colors and patterns, and it has an inherent beauty that is impossible to match. The general category of woods that the interior designer is interested is called "hardwoods." It has been said that there are about 99,000 different species of hardwoods throughout the world, but only about 250 are commercially available. Of these, the following are perhaps the best known:

Afromosia
Ambera

Ash, brown
Ash, white

Aspen
Avodire
Basswood
Beech, American
Benge
Birch, natural
Birch, white
Bosse (African cedar)
Bubinga
Butternut
Cedar, aromatic
Cherry, American
Cherry, foreign
Chestnut, English
Chestnut, wormy
Cypress
Ebony, Macassar
Elm, Carpathian
Elm, American brown
Gum, red
Goncalo, alves (tiger wood or zebra wood)
Hackberry
Harewood, English
Hickory
Honey
Kmbuya
Koa
Kokrodua
"Korina" (limba)
Lauan, red
Lauan, white
Lacewood
Laredo (breadnut)
Laurel, East Indian
Mahogany, African
Mahogany, Honduras
Makore (African cherry)
Minzu

Maple
Myrtle
Narra
Oak, American
Oak, English
Oak, brown
Oak, red
Oak, white
Orientalwood
Padouk, Burma
Paldao
Persimmon
Pearwood, Swiss
Primavera
Pecan
Poplar, yellow
Rosewood, Brazilian
Rosewood, Madagascar
Rosewood, East Indian
Sapele
Satinwood
Silkwood
Sycamore, American
Sycamore, English
Tupelo (gum)
Teak, African
Teak, Burmese
Tola
Tamo (Japanese ash)
Thuya
Tigerwood
Tulipwood
Vermilion
Walnut, American
Walnut, European
Walnut, Rhodesian
Wenge
Yew, English

An examination of various kinds of wood shows a wide spectrum of colors from pale yellow pink through pink and medium pale yellow to brownish orange, pinkish brown, reddish brown, black brown, and almond (see Plate VI). The color varies according to the species. Beauty and additional variation may be obtained in veneers by creating "figure," which is determined by the species of the tree, the cutting method, and the part of the tree from which the veneer is cut (see Figure 5.4).

Plywood is made by laminating three or more layers of wood with adhesives. The face ply is the veneer that is to be seen. The center ply is called the core, and the ply immediately adjacent to the face ply is called a "crossband." Plywood construction may have three, five, seven, or any other odd number of plies. The grain of each layer is laid at right angles to the grain of the adjacent ply. The face ply can be cut in several ways— plain slicing, quarter slicing, rotary, half-round, and rift cut. Depending upon the type of wood used, additional patterns and figures can be obtained. Some of them are listed below (see Plate VII):

Patterns:	Pencil stripe	Figures:	Stumpwood
	Fiddleback		Feather crotch
	Mottled		Crotch swirl
	Blistered		Birdseye
			Crossfire
			Ribbon stripe

Further variation can be obtained by the manner in which the wood is matched. Veneers may be selected for a particular kind of graining, then joined together within a panel to produce various figures (see Figure 5.5): diamond, reverse diamond, box, reverse box, checkerboard, and herringbone. Book match is obtained by turning over alternate sheets of a flitch in the manner of opening a book. (A flitch is a section of a tree that has been sliced and kept together. More than one flitch can be cut from a large tree.) Slip match is obtained by placing adjacent sheets of veneer side by side without turning. (It is also called slide match). Center match is obtained by placing an equal number of sheets with the same pattern on each side of a center line. Running match (or lot match) is obtained when veneers are laid up in the same sequence as they occupy in the flitch. Excess veneer from the first panel is used to begin the second panel; excess veneer from the second panel is used to begin the third panel, and so on.

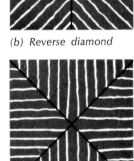

(a) Diamond   (b) Reverse diamond

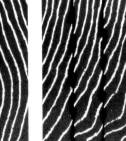

(a) Book match   (b) Slip match

(c) Box   (d) Reverse box

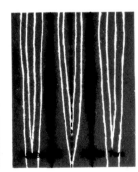

(c) Center match   (d) Running match

FIG. 5.5 Methods of matching plywood

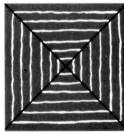
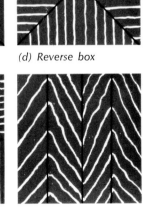
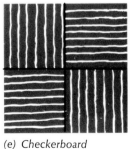

(e) Checkerboard   (f) Herringbone

FIG. 5.4 Different types of matching plywood

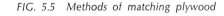
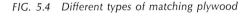

The average woodwork mill stocks a fairly limited number of woods. A number of companies produce stock plywood paneling which varies in price from inexpensive to moderately expensive. The range of woods available depends on their popularity; only a relatively small number of plywoods can be stocked. Among those most commonly available are wormy chestnut, birch, Salem Korina, pecan, butternut, walnut, persimmon, red oak, rosewood, cherry, teak, birch, elm, and hickory. In addition to natural finishes, a number of "tortured" finishes are available in several colors. These are made by sandblasting the face of a panel, thereby eroding the soft grain and leaving the harder grain in relief.

In addition to the foregoing commercially available plywoods, certain solid wood panels are also obtainable. These are V-jointed and the sides and ends are tongue and groove. They are available in several species and grades, as well as various widths and lengths. The following selections are offered by the Townsend Lumber Company:

Species	Thickness (in.)	Grade	Finish	
Ash	1/2	Select[a]	Prefinished & Unfinished	
		Colonial[b]	"	"
Birch	1/2	Select	Prefinished	
Cherry[e]	1/2	Select	Prefinished & Unfinished	
		Colonial	"	"
Delta Marble	1/2	Select	"	"
Maple	1/2	Antique	"	"
Red Oak[d, e]	1/2	Select	"	"
		Colonial	"	"
Walnut[e]	1/2	Select	"	"
		Wattled[c]	"	"
Willow	1/2	Select	"	"
		Colonial	"	"
Cypress	3/4	Pecky	"	"

[a] Without knots.

[b] With knots.

[c] Wattled wood is made from hardwoods selected for natural characteristics, such as burls, bird pecks, worm holes, sound knots, etc.

[d] Also available in specially selected 3/4-in., prefinished, light- and dark-toned panels ("Carriage House Paneling," which comes in white oak too).

[e] Also available in some grades in textured treatment ("Roughsawn").

Widths include 4, 5, 6, 7 and 8 in., except 1/2-in. oak, which comes in 4-, 5-, and 6-in. widths only and pecky cypress, which is available in 6-, 8-, 10- and 12-in. widths; 35 to 50 per cent of panels are 8 ft. 0 in. in length, with the balance in combinations of 8 ft. 0 in. Combinations in longer lengths are available on special order.

The architect or interior designer will in most cases wish to personally select the paneling that is to go into an installation. In many cases he will be able to see both plywood and solid panels at a local showroom. However, if the job is an important one he will probably visit a showroom such as that of William L. Marshall, Ltd. in New York City where he may select the desired veneer for length, color and grain.

Let us assume that the designer wishes to use Brazilian rosewood. In the showroom he will be shown samples of wood from which he can make his selection. He will find that most of the color in the wood will vary from yellow to a pinkish gray. Each ply in the bale will be numbered to indicate its relative position in the tree before it was sliced—for example, 1-3, 2-3, or 3-3. As many as eight representative samples will be kept for each flitch. The best wood is cut into veneers, since more good face wood can be obtained from a tree in this manner. Defective wood is sold as lumber.

When the flitches have been selected, they are sent to the plywood-manufacturing company. When a flitch has been sold, the sample of it in the showroom is cut for general-use samples to prevent the possibility that it may be shown to another client.

Generally speaking, the flitches shown in the showroom are unfinished, and the finishing process is chosen by the architect or interior designer. However, it is recommended that a material which does not hide the grain (such as water-soluble stains or lacquer) be used rather than oil stains, which tend to hide the grain of the wood.

In addition to the usual methods of using wood, a number of "banded" woods are made by gluing together several plies of two different colors. For example, wood panels made by the "fine-line process," which is popular in Europe, are made by gluing together bands of light and dark plywood sheets. When these sheets have been glued together in a log, they are sliced vertically into panels; the light and dark wood shows as a pattern on the face of each panel. The pattern can be varied as desired by varying the distance between the dark sheets.

With all the different kinds and colors of wood available, the color selection for any given job might seem to be complicated beyond belief. However, the same set of principles described in Chapter 2 on color theory can be used here. Look closely at a piece of walnut, and you will see that it is not all one color, but several colors. The background may vary from reddish brown to yellow brown, while the graining may be blue brown. Therefore it is safe to say that walnut has in it red, yellow, and blue. If the wood has a yellow cast, it is obvious that yellow is one of the colors that may be used with it. Zebrawood falls into this category. An examination will show that it contains yellow (chrome yellow), red (an alizarin crimson), and blue (a french ultramarine). By mixing these three colors, plus white, the color of zebrawood can be obtained. This fact means that any of these three colors may be used alone or in combination in varying amounts to complement zebrawood.

When the color of unfinished teak is analyzed optically, it will be found to contain yellow ochre, vermilion, and cobalt blue. The colors in a pinkish rosewood will be yellow ochre, alizarin crimson, and a french ultramarine blue. If one wall in a paneled room is to be painted, there are several color options. It can, of course, be painted a color similar to the general tone of the wood, in a lighter or darker shade. It may be painted any of the colors that are found in the optical analysis of the wood. A color complementary to the general tone of the wood may be used; for instance, if a wood such as teak has a yellow-orange cast, a shade of blue violet, its complement, may be used with it. Analogous colors, such as orange and yellow, may also be used. One of the triads containing yellow orange may be employed. A good triad would be a scheme of yellow orange, red violet, and blue green, or a split complement using a yellow orange and perhaps a violet and a blue.

Obviously, with an expenditure as great as that which would be required for the use of an exotic wood brought from some far corner of the earth, color studies illustrating all of the colors and textures to be used in the room, as well as a good colored perspective drawing, should be made before any of the materials are ordered.

Plastic Laminates

Of all the plastics that are available to the architect and interior designer, plastic laminates are perhaps the best known and most widely used. Essentially these are made of extremely hard and durable plastic that is mounted as a veneer on plywood or other board. Used on walls, counters, table tops, and furniture, they resist alcohol and staining by alkalis or acids (see Figure 5.6). A special quality is available for use where cigarette burns are likely to occur.

Plastic laminates (or high-pressure laminated plastic material) are produced by several manufacturers, each of whom has various colors, patterns, and finishes. The Formica Corporation produces four basic finishes:

Furniture: A semigloss finish, achieved by a special machining of the surface, for both horizontal and vertical surfaces

Suede: Minutely grained texture with low reflective surface, for both horizontal and vertical surfaces

Polished: A high-gloss finish specially suited to applications where maximum smoothness and luster are desired, usually for horizontal surfaces

M Finish: A semigloss finish specially developed for stain resistance, usually for horizontal surfaces

The number of finishes available for solid colors, patterns, and wood grains varies, as not every finish is available for every color. Other manufacturers may give their finishes other names. Some of these are listed below:

Consoweld (Consoweld Corp.)
Formica (Formica Corp.)
Melamite (Melamite Corp.)
Micarta (Westinghouse Corp.)
Nevamar (Nevamar Co.)
Parkwood (Parkwood Laminates, Inc.)
Pionite (Pioneer Plastics Corp.)
Textolite (General Electric, Laminated Products Dept.)
Wilson-Art (Ralph Wilson Plastics, Inc.)

FIG. 5.6 The use of laminated plastic: teakwood grain on walls, red on Oriental chest

Formica provides lines of solid colors, colored patterns, wood-grain patterns, and special designs. Sheets are available in widths of 24, 30, 36, 48, and 60 inches, and lengths of 60, 72, 84, 96, 120, and 144 inches. Different grades are recommended for special requirements. There is 1/16-inch Standard Grade for both horizontal and vertical applications; Postforming 0.050 inches to permit small radii bending for use with commercial postforming equipment; and V-32 for the vertical surfaces of cabinets. Solid colors available are:

White	Persimmon
Antique White	Signal Red
Putty Gray	Flame
Champagne	Bittersweet
Gray	Pumpkin
Beige	Terra Cotta
Dove	Primrose
Fawn	Lemon Twist
Sagebrush	Butterscotch
Cocoa	Buckskin
Charcoal	Chutney
Umber	Absinthe
Seal	Green Olive
Black	Midi
Matador	Caribbean Blue
Aqua	French Blue
Light Aqua	Concord
Lime	Grape
Celadon	Heather
Frost Green	Camellia
Emerald	Rasberry
Azure	Wild Plum

Patterns are as follows (these are all small-scale and delicate):

Linen:	Designed to simulate linen fabric. Green, Gray, Primrose, Tan, Lipstick
Willow:	A series of interconnected colored lines which simulate bare tree branches on pale ground. Pink, Beige, Yellow, Green, Blue
Spindrift:	Flecks of gold and graining on colored background. Camellia, Light Aqua, White, Champagne
Sequin:	Random flecks of gold on colored background. Champagne, White
Marble:	Pink Lioz, Gray Lioz, Antique Lioz, Gray Frost, Portugese Lioz, Classic Cremo, Beige Frost
Fernglo:	Small flowers on a linenlike background. Blue, Green, Beige, Yellow, Gray
Finesse:	An overall random tracing of colored lines on a light background. Moonwhite, Sauterne, Candlelight, Cantaloupe
Mayflower:	A series of colored abstract flowers in a geometric pattern on a light background. Yellow, White
Pinwheel:	A series of interlocking circles made of colored dots on a neutral background. White

Wood grain patterns available are:

Rift Sliced White Oak	Fruitwood
Birch	Sequoia Redwood
Prima Vera	Spanish Oak
Golden Maple	Royal Walnut
Plain Sliced White Oak	Modern Walnut
Cortena Pecan	Flat Cut Centurion Walnut
White Tidewood	Flat Cut Malacca Teak
Island Driftwood	Flat Cut Regency Walnut
Honey Tone Oak	Barnwood
Burnt Sugar Maple	Frost Walnut
Cherry	Tawny Walnut
Tropical Rosewood	Rosewood
Paldao	Macassar Ebony
Flat Cut Provincial Cherry	Ribbon Stripe African Mahogany
Flat Cut English Oak	

Special designs covering a range from broken stripes, fretwork, and mosaic to damask and lace patterns are available in one, two, or three colors and a background color.

Because of the popularity of plastic laminates, manufacturers are striving constantly to produce new effects and colors. While many colors and patterns remain standard, others change from year to year.

Stone

Because of its beautiful color and texture, stone is often used in interior work. Its weight poses support problems, but they can sometimes be solved by cutting the stone into rather thin sheets and anchoring or cementing them to a wall or partition. This can be done only when the face of each stone is to be relatively flat.

Many kinds of stone are available, and many kinds come in various colors—whites, yellows, oranges, browns, and grays. The tonal variation of each kind is usually subtle; most people think of a stone wall as being gray or brown. A close visual analysis of such a wall, however, will reveal an unsuspected number of color variations. The color variations of stone must be taken into consideration when one selects colors to be used near it.

Ideally the stone to be used should be collected either from the site of a proposed building or from adjoining areas; however, even if it is present in sufficient quantity, the cost of gathering and the cutting of such stone is often so great that it is uneconomical to use local stone for interior work. Suppliers of stone can provide a wide variety which may be selected from sample display walls laid in various patterns. See Plate VIII for a representative list.

1. Colorado stone—random ashlar pattern
2. Lava stone—rubble pattern
3. Georgia crystal white marble—sawed-bed ashlar pattern
4. Pennsylvania mica—sawed-bed ashlar pattern
5. Turquoise stone—rubble mosaic pattern
6. Pine log—rubble mosaic pattern

Following is a list of stones and their color ranges. These are split-face ashlar and rubble veneers, most of which are 4 inches thick; some are heavier, some lighter.

In some applications, sawed-bed materials which do not have a concave face can be cut down, usually to a 1-inch thickness, and slotted to receive aluminum anchoring clips. This 1-inch veneer can be applied on any surface material, but cement board is best. The joints are usually about 1/2 inch and are pointed with cement. When the joints are filled it is, of course, impossible to tell how thick the veneer is. Local sources, or the Building Stone Institute (420 Lexington Ave., New York, N.Y.), may be contacted for further information.

Stone Name	Color	Quarry Location	Availability
Adirondack hue	Predominantly lavender pink; buff to gray	N.Y.	Eastern U.S.
Argillite	Deep brown to purple to blue; some gray and buff	N.J.	U.S.
Austone:	Light cream to buff	Tex.	U.S.
Cordova creme			
Cordova shell			
Bluestone	Blue gray to gray green, some rust	N.Y., Pa.	Eastern U.S.
Briar Hill	Buff, beige to red burgundy	Ohio	U.S.
Brownstone (reclaimed)	Light to medium brown	From de-molished buildings	N.Y. area
Brownstone (quarried)	Light to medium brown	Mass.	U.S.
Cactus Canyon:		Ariz. and Calif.	U.S.
Turquoise	Russet and lilac; some blue green		
Green	Light green, white spots		
Carolina granite:		N.C.	U.S.
Rowan pink	Gray white to pale gray pink		
Balfour pink	Reddish pink to pale pink		
Salisbury	Orange pink		
Chesapeake hue	Gray, buff, brown, rust	Del.	Eastern U.S.
Clark Island granite	Gray to rust	Maine	Eastern U.S.
Colorado stone	Light pink to deep rose	Colo.	U.S.
Coral rock	Light beige	Fla.	U.S.
Cold Spring granite	Eighteen varieties, all colors	Minn.	U.S.
Delaware sandstone	Browns, grays, and russet	Pa.	U.S.
Delaware fieldstone	Tans, gray, brown, rose, and beige	Pa.	U.S.
Desert onyx	White to pale peach	Utah	U.S.
Desert Hills	Rust on beige to gray	Midwest	U.S.
Featherock	Gray, charcoal, tan to light brown	Calif.	U.S.
Georgia granite:		Ga.	U.S.
Blue diamond	Gray white with dark specks		
Congaree	Light gray with large black specks		
Kershaw pink	Pale pink with large black specks		
Georgia marble:	White, gray, black and white, pink, pink to gray white	Ga.	U.S.
Crystal white			
Pink etowah			
Creole			
Cherokee			
Variegated			
Golden green	Medium green	Pa.	U.S.
Green range	Medium green to rust	Pa.	U.S.
Hymar ebony	Black with white and rust	N.C.	U.S.
Lava	Deep brown to charcoal	N.Mex.	U.S.
Lenroc	Blue gray, some brown and rust	N.Y.	Eastern U.S.
Limestone:	Buff to gray with veining	Ala.	U.S.
Alabama			

Stone Name	Color	Quarry Location	Availability
Limestone: Indiana	Gray to buff	Ind.	U.S.
Limestone: Minnesota	Cream, gray, pink, red maroon, buff tones	Minn.	U.S.
Pennsylvania mica	Silvery gray to gold	Pa.	U.S.
Pine log	Ivory, orange, tan, gray, blue, brown and rust tones	Ga.	U.S.
Sienna sandstone	Red, pink, brown, tan, yellow, and buff	Ind.	U.S.
Sea mist	All shades green to gray, mica sparkles	Canada	U.S.
Silver satin	Light to dark gray, mica sparkles		U.S.
Sunset	Medium to dark pink, mica sparkles	Canada	U.S.
Shadowrock	Beige, tan, brown, orange	Pa.	U.S.
Snow Mountain	White with green, lavender	N.C.	U.S.
Stone Mountain granite	Gray white with flecks	Ga.	U.S.
Tennessee stone	Tan, orange, medium to dark brown veining	Tenn.	U.S.
Tennessee marble	Pink to gray; medium to dark cedar	Tenn.	U.S.
Turquoise stone	Pale green to turquoise	Utah	U.S.
Vermont marble, Green Mountain quarry:		Vt.	U.S.
Emerald white	White with green		
Emerald green	Green with white		
Sunset blue	Blue gray		
Watauga stone:		N.C.	U.S.
Watauga green	Medium to deep green with white spots		
Watauga orchid	Medium purple with white spots		
Westchester granite	Dark to medium blue gray, some pink	N.Y.	Eastern U.S.
Weymouth granite	Gray, tan, rust	Mass.	U.S.

Marble

Marble, a crystalline stone, is the result of pressure, heat, and contact with mineral-bearing waters upon limestone. It has a fine, dense texture and takes an excellent polish. Marble varies in color and pattern according to the location in which it is formed. The wide range of colors is caused by the presence in greater or lesser amounts of carbonaceous matter, oxides of iron, graphite, mica, and silica; these ingredients also contribute to the types of grain, or pattern, which is found in the various kinds of marble. Some marble is relatively soft and can be used for interior work only. Hard marble, of course, may be used for interior as well as exterior work. Because of the great expense that the quarrying, cutting, shaping, and finishing of marble entails, marble is today confined to work of major importance. The cost can be brought down by cutting it into thing sheets (say 1 1/4 inches) and mounting it on interior masonry walls or partitions. Like that of wood, its beauty is in its varying color and pattern. No two pieces are exactly alike, and their variation, as well as the rich appearance that marble produces, provides a highly desired dignity.

Marble can be given several different finishes: polished, honed, sand-rubbed, or abrasive. While smooth finishes tend, in general, to emphasize color and veining, the rougher finishes tend to subdue veinings or markings. Sawn, tooled, axed, and other finishes are available on special order.

Color Ranges of 311 Marbles Currently in Production

Domestic

Black

(B) Imperial Black .... Imperial
(A) Radio Black .... Vermont
(A) Virginia Alberene Black
 Serpentine .... Alberene

Blue gray

(A) Minnesota Skyrose Fleuri .... Vetter
(B) Minnesota Skyrose Veine .... Vetter
(A) Sunset Blue .... Green Mountain

Buff-brown-yellowish

(A) Buff Kasota Fleuri .... Babcock
(A) Buff Kasota Veine .... Babcock
(C) Cliffdale .... Carthage
(C) Colocreme .... Carthage
(A) Cream Man-Sota Fleuri .... Babcock
(A) Cream Man-Sota Veine .... Babcock
(C) Golden Melange .... Carthage
(A) Ka-Kato Cream Fleuri .... Vetter
(A) Mankato Buff .... Mankato
(B) Mankato Cream .... Mankato
(A) Minnesota Golden Buff Fleuri .... Vetter
(A) Minnesota Golden Buff Veine .... Vetter
(A) Minnesota Travernelle .... Vetter
(A) Northern Cream Fleuri .... Vetter
(A) Northern Cream Veine .... Vetter
(C) Onyx Antigua .... Antigua
(A) Spring Mist .... Victor Oolitic
(C) St. Clair Golden Vein .... Carthage
(C) Ste. Genevieve Golden Vein .... Tennessee
(C) Temple Creme Travertine .... Ultra
(A) Vetter Kasota Cream Fleuri .... Vetter
(A) Vetter Kasota Cream Veine .... Vetter
(A) V.O. Travertine .... Victor Oolitic

Gray

(A) Carthage Exterior Marble .... Carthage
(A) Carthage Patina Vein .... Carthage
(A) Carthage Texture Vein .... Carthage
(A) Georgia Mezzotint .... Nelson
(A) Gray Danby .... Vermont
(A) Gray Kasota Fleuri .... Babcock
(A) Gray Kasota Veine .... Babcock
(A) Mankato Gray .... Mankato
(A) Minnesota Pearl Gray Fleuri .... Vetter
(A) Minnesota Pearl Gray Veine .... Vetter
(A) Minnesota Silver Gray Fleuri .... Vetter
(A) Napoleon Gray .... Carthage
(A) Northern Gray Fleuri .... Vetter
(A) Northern Gray Veine .... Vetter
(A) Ozark Fleuri .... Carthage
(A) Ozark Gray Veined .... Carthage
(A) Ozark Tavernelle .... Carthage
(A) Silvetto .... Carthage
(C) Suprema Delta Gray
 Veined Alabama .... Colonna
(C) Suprema Delta
 Hazeltone Alabama .... Colonna
(A) Vermarco Cadet Gray .... Vermont
(A) Vermarco Florence .... Vermont
(A) Vermarco Neshobe Gray Clouded . Vermont
(A) Vermarco Neshobe Gray Veined .. Vermont

Grayish pink

(A) Rose Gray .... Tennessee

Green

(C) Maryland Verde, Antique . Maryland Green
(A) Vermarco Jademar .... Vermont
(A) Vermarco Pico Green .... Vermont
(A) Vermarco Taconic Green Vein .... Vermont
(C) Vermarco Verde Antique .... Vermont

Light green

(A) Vermarco Brocadillo .... Vermont
(A) Vermarco Listavena .... Vermont
(A) Vermarco Olivo .... Vermont
(A) Vermarco Pavonazzo .... Vermont
(A) Vermarco Striped Brocadillo ...... Vermont
(A) Vert Mont .... Green Mountain

Pink

(A) Endsley Pink .... Tennessee
(A) Georgia Etowah Pink .... Nelson
(A) Minnesota Pink Fleuri .... Babcock
(A) Minnesota Pink Fleuri .... Vetter
(A) Minnesota Pink Veine .... Babcock
(A) Minnesota Pink Veine .... Vetter
(A) Northern Pink Buff Fleuri .... Vetter
(A) Northern Pink Buff Veine .... Vetter
(A) Pink Buff Kasota Fleuri .... Babcock
(A) Pink Buff Kasota Veine .... Babcock
(A) Pink Caroline Fleuri .... Babcock
(A) Pink Caroline Veine .... Babcock
(A) Pink Man-Sota Fleuri .... Babcock
(A) Pink Man-Sota Veine .... Babcock
(A) Pink Marquette Fleuri .... Babcock
(A) Pink Marquette Veine .... Babcock
(A) Rose Tavernelle .... Tennessee
(A) Temain Pink .... Tennessee
(A) Vetter Kasota Pink Fleuri .... Vetter
(A) Vetter Kasota Pink Veine .... Vetter

Red to reddish brown

(C) Breccia .... Ultra
(A) Cedar Tavernelle .... Tennessee
(C) Colorosa Mahogany .... Carthage
(C) Colorosa Travertine .... Carthage
(A) Mahogany Antique .... Tennessee
(C) Ozark Famosa .... Carthage
(C) Ozark Rouge .... Carthage
(A) Rouge Fossile .... Tennessee
(C) Royal Breche .... Carthage
(A) Veined Cedar .... Tennessee

Rose

(C) Ozark Crystal Rose .... Carthage
(C) Rose Agate .... Carthage
(C) Rose Cecile .... Carthage
(A) Rose Fleuri .... Babcock
(A) Rose Veine .... Babcock
(C) Scheherazade .... Ultra
(C) Ste. Genevieve Breche Rose ..... Tennessee
(C) Ste. Genevieve Rose .... Tennessee

White

(A) Amco White .... Alabama
(A) Imperial Danby .... Vermont
(A) Vermarco Best Light Cloud .... Vermont
(A) Vermarco Statuary .... Vermont
(A) Vermarco Taconic White .... Vermont

Color Ranges of 311 Marbles Currently in Production *(Cont.)*

White, bluish

(A) Amco Pantellic White...........Alabama
(A) Corona Danby...................Vermont
(A) Dorset White...........Green Mountain
(A) Georgia Creole....................Nelson
(A) Georgia White Cherokee..........Nelson
(A) Highland Danby.................Vermont
(A) Royal Danby....................Vermont

White, brownish

(A) Eureka Danby...................Vermont

White, creamy

(A) Alabama Delta White...........Colonna
(A) Amco Cream....................Alabama

(A) Amco Cream Cloud..............Alabama
(A) Regal White Danby..............Vermont

White, greenish

(A) Mariposa Clouded Danby.........Vermont
(A) Mariposa Veined Danby..........Vermont
(A) Meadow White..........Green Mountain
(A) Meadow White Fleuri....Green Mountain
(A) Montclair Danby..................Vermont
(A) Plateau Danby...................Vermont
(A) Vermarco Crinkly Vein..........Vermont
(A) Vermarco Light Cloud...........Vermont
(A) Vermarco Mottled White.........Vermont

Yellow or Gold

(C) Desert Gold Travertine..............Ultra

Foreign

(Belgium, Italy, Spain, Mexico, France, Morocco, Canada, Yugoslavia, Portugal, Turkey,
Greece, Sweden, Rumania, Iran, England, Switzerland, Peru)

Black

(D) Belgian Black....................Belgium
(D) Black and Gold.....................Italy
(D) Blue Beige......................Belgium
(B) Gris Antique....................Belgium
(C) Gris Arratia.......................Spain
(C) Mino Nero Antique..............Mexico
(C) Negro Marquina...................Spain
(C) Noir Izeste......................France
(A) Petit Granit (not a granite)........Belgium
(D) Portoveer (black and white)...........Italy
(C) Ste. Anne African Vein...........Morocco
(D) Ste. Laurent (Pyrenees
          black and white)..............France

Blue-White (white with blue cast)

(B) Rideau Blue Dark.................Canada
(A) Rideau Blue Fleuri...............Canada

Brecciated (black and white)

(C) Breche Rencesvalles (all types)......France
(C) Roman Breche (Breche Noire)......France

Brown

(B) Antique Fleuri.................Yugoslavia
(C) Breche Nouvelle...................France
(C) Cremo Nuevo.....................Spain
(C) Notre Dame Lunel.................France
(C) Travertine Andrea...................Italy
(C) Travertine Este Dark.................Italy
(D) Travertine Geneva Antique..........Italy
(C) Travertine Oniciato.................Italy
(C) Travertine St. Peter.................Italy
(D) Travertine Walnut..................Italy

Buff, cream or light

(C) Botticino..........................Italy
(B) Hauteville......................France
(C) Ivory Vein (light and dark)..........Spain
(C) Lioz Cream....................Portugal
(D) Loredo Chiaro Light (Alba Pallido)...Italy
(C) Loredo Rubane....................Italy
(C) Notre Dame.....................France
(C) Perlato D'Italia (Cream Perla)
          (Dolcetta Perloto)...............Italy

(C) Santa Clara.........................Spain
(B) Selje Cream...................Yugoslavia
(C) Tavernelle Medium..................Italy
(C) Travertine Almond..................Italy
(C) Travertine Annabella................Italy
(C) Travertine Este Light...............Italy
(C) Travertine Geneva Cream
          (Tuscan Light)..................Italy
(D) Travertine Imperial (all types)........Italy
(C) Travertine Palm....................Italy
(C) Travertine Roman...................Italy
(C) Travertine Roman Light.............Italy

Buff, Dark

(C) Botticino Dark (all types)............Italy
(C) Rubane..........................France

Gray

(B) Aurisina (all types)..................Italy
(B) Gray Alhambra.....................Spain

Gray, bluish

(A) Bardiglietto........................Italy
(B) Blue Argentato.....................Italy
(C) Crystal Blue....................Portugal
(B) Mamora Vein......................Turkey

Green

(C) Campan Rose Vert.................France
(B) Cipollino Verde Apuano.............Italy
(C) Forest Green (all types).............Italy
(D) Greek Cipollino...................Greece
(C) Monte Verde (Verde Aver)...........Italy
(C) Moss Green Serpentine..............Italy
(C) Serpentine Scuro...................Italy
(C) Sirocco Green......................Italy
(C) Swedish Green.................Sweden
(C) Tinos............................Greece
(D) Verde Alpi (Alps green).............Italy
(C) Verde Antonio......................Italy
(C) Verde Imperial.....................Italy
(C) Verde Issorie......................Italy
(C) Verde Lenco.......................Italy
(C) Verde Polcevera....................Italy
(C) Ver-Myen Serpentine...............Italy

Color Ranges of 311 Marbles Currently in Production (*Cont.*)

(C) Vert Christina ....Italy
(C) Vert d'Estours ....France
(C) Vert Floran ....Italy
(C) Vert Racega ....Italy
(C) Vert Ste. Anna ....Italy
(C) Verte Jade ....Portugal

Red

(C) Languedoc.......................France
(C) Ramello Rosso ....Italy
(C) Red Antique of Italy...............Italy
(D) Red Levanto ....Italy
(C) Red Verona ....Italy
(C) Rojo Alicante (Red Altico)..........Spain
(C) Rojo Ereno ....Spain
(C) Rojo Toreador ....Spain
(B) Rose Vif (Rouge d'Ariege)
       (Rose Hortensia) ....France
(C) Rosso Alberato ....Italy
(C) Rosso Magnaboschi...................Italy
(D) Rosso Mandina (Rosso Collemandina).Italy
(C) Rosso Merlino (Rouge Incarnat) ....France
(C) Rouge De Neuville...............Belgium
(C) Rouge Fleuri.....................Rumania
(C) Rouge Matador ....Spain
(C) Rouge Royal (all types) ....Belgium
(C) Travertine Sunset Red ....Iran

Rose

(C) Almiscado ....Portugal
(C) Bilbao Reale ....Spain
(D) Cassino Rose ....Italy
(C) Coral Pink...........................Italy
(C) Cunard Pink (Chiampo Porfirico) ......Italy
(C) Duquesa (Rose Turquesa)...........Spain
(B) Norwegian Rose ....Norway
(D) Rosa Corallo (Coral Pink) ....Italy
(C) Rosalit.........................Yugoslavia
(C) Rose Alhambra ....Spain
(C) Rose Espanol ....Spain
(C) Rose St. Xavier ....France
(D) Rosora (Tuscan Rose) ....Italy
(C) St. Florient Rose ....Portugal
(C) Tavernelle Perlatto....................Italy
(C) Tavernelle Rose Fleuri................Italy

Veined and/or brecciated
(bluish or gray background)

(B) African Gris Lilas ....Morocco
(C) Bardiglio (veined types) ....Italy
(C) Bois Jourdan ....France
(B) Fior di Mare.........................Italy
(D) Firo di Pesco Carnico (all types) .....Italy
(D) Fleur de Peche (classic type) ....Italy
(C) Gris Perle ....Morocco
(C) Gris Perle Rose ....Morocco
(C) Italian Gray ....Italy
(C) Lido (all types) ....Morocco
(C) Platina Gris ....Morocco
(C) Platina Rose....................Morocco
(D) Renfrew.........................England
(C) Repoveco ....Yugoslavia
(C) Ruvina (Ruivina) ....Portugal
(B) Ste. Anne Beaux Arts...............France
(B) Ste. Anne Des Pyrenees ....France

Veined and/or brecciated
(cream or white background)

(B) Arabescato (all types) ....Italy
(C) Balacet ....France
(A) Bettogli Vein ....Italy
(B) Breche Fantasia ....Italy
(C) Breche Rosato ....Italy
(D) Breche Violet.......................Italy
(C) Calacata (all types) ....Italy
(C) Cremo Delicato ....Italy
(A) English Vein Italian ....Italy
(C) Escalette Alpha ....France
(C) Escalette Balacet ....France
(A) Gioia Vein ....Italy
(C) Golden Vein Paonazzo..............Italy
(C) Iride Fiorito ....Italy
(C) Italian Cremo (classic) ....Italy
(C) Italian Cremo Rose Veined ....Italy
(C) Italian Skyros ....Italy
(B) Lasa White (clouded or veined).......Italy
(C) Mexican Onyx (all types)..........Mexico
(C) Paonazetto ....Italy
(D) Paonazzo (all types) ....Italy
(C) Pedrara Onyx ....Mexico
(C) Piastraccia ....Italy
(C) Rose Aurora ....Portugal
(C) Rose Portas ....Portugal
(C) Skyros Rose ....Morocco
(C) Statuario Zebrino ....Italy
(B) Statuary Vein (all types) ....Italy
(C) Verde Fantastico ....Italy
(C) Vergados ....Portugal

Veined and/or brecciated
(tan or yellowish background)

(C) Breche Aurora ....Italy
(C) Crema Moderno ....Spain
(C) Filetto Rosso........................Italy
(C) Jaune de Portugal (Jaune Ste. Rose).Portugal
       (Rose Ste. Jean) ....Portugal
       (St. Antonio) (St. Sylvester) .....Portugal
(D) Loredo Ciaro (all types) ....Italy
(C) Loredo Zani ....Italy
(D) Macchiavecchia...............Switzerland
(C) Ondagata (Serpeggiante) ....Italy
(C) Rosato............................Italy
(C) Rose de Brignoles ....France
(C) Travertine Etruscan (all types) ....Italy

White

(B) Blanco De Nieve...............Yugoslavia
(A) Blanco P (all types) ....Italy
(B) Aegean Crystal ....Greece
(A) Lasa White (select) ....Italy
(A) Rideau White ....Canada
(A) White Carrara (Bianco Chiaro) ....Italy

Yellow or Gold

(D) Aztec Onyx.......................Mexico
(C) Crema Espanol ....Spain
(D) Siena (all types) ....Italy
(C) Travertine Golden (light and dark).....Italy
(C) Travertine Imperial Golden..........Spain
(C) Travertine Peruvian Golden (all types) .Peru
(C) Yellow Verona (all types) ....Italy

Source: Marble Forecast 1967, Marble Institute of America, Inc., Washington, D.C.

Following are descriptions of the classifications indicated in the foregoing list, as set up by the Marble Institute of America:

Group A   Sound marbles and stones with uniform and favorable working qualities.

Group B   Marbles and stones similar in character to the preceding group, but working qualities somewhat less favorable; occasional natural faults; a limited amount of waxing and sticking is necessary.

Group C   Marbles and stones with some variations in working qualities; geological flaws, voids, veins, and lines of separation are common. It is standard shop practice to repair these variations by sticking, waxing, and filling. Liners and other forms of reinforcement are employed when necessary.

Group D   Marbles and stones similar to the preceding group, but containing a larger proportion of natural faults and a maximum variation in working qualities, thus requiring more finishing. This group comprises many of the highly colored marbles prized for their decorative qualities.

Limestone is made up of small round grains of carbonate of lime or the remains of skeletons and shells of marine animals. In color it varies from white to gray, cream, or yellowish brown. Sometimes the texture is smooth; sometimes it is pitted by the fossilized remains of sea life.

Travertine is a limestone that has been made porous by running water. It is often used in interior work.

It is wise to examine marble (or any other natural material) before purchasing it. The architect or interior designer should visit the yard of the marble contractor, examine the stock for color and graining, and obtain samples before ordering.

Mirrors

Mirrors in the most primitive form were made of polished bronze in ancient Egypt and ancient Greece. In Greece they were so expensive and highly valued that usually their protective cover was finely decorated. During the Italian Renaissance, Venice, the center of the ornamental-glass industry, produced small wall mirrors. Like the hand mirrors of ancient times, they were protected, usually with a wood panel or door, and their frames were also highly decorated. The convex mirror was an invention of the sixteenth century. The modern mirror is a sheet of clear, polished plate glass silvered with a solution of ammonia and silver nitrate. The silvering, which would otherwise decompose in the presence of dampness, is protected with a coat of varnish or shellac and a double coat of lead or of tar paint. Sometimes the silver back is covered by an electrostatically applied layer of copper. The rarity and costliness of mirrors was acknowledged in the past by their magnificent carved-wood and pierced-metal frames. A small hand mirror, reflecting only a small image, is practical when it is in use, and ornamental in itself. Wall-hung mirrors, whose function is primarily decorative, are back-coated with dull silver, gold chloride, or lead to give interesting graining, smoky patterns, the appearance of patterned gold metal, or a marbleized effect of, say, black, white, and gold. The appearance of mirrors may also be modified by using tinted plate glass in neutral gray or bronze hues.

Improvements in manufacturing methods have made large mirrors possible. Used in a contemporary interior, large mirrors are designed to reflect not only the image but the color and pattern of areas around it (see Figure 5.7). A small area may be made to

appear larger by using expanses of mirror on one wall. Mirrored ceilings, reflecting all things below, create interesting effects. Block mirrors, made of a series of beveled mirror forms, not only reflect things around them but give scale and pattern to a room. A large mirror composed of small units is less expensive and easier to ship and install than a single mirror of the same size.

FIG. 5.7 Block mirrors installed on wall of dining area

Ceramic Tile

The word "tile" is all-inclusive. It covers the painted and decorated glazed tiles of ancient Egypt, Assyria, Babylonia, and Persia, the decorative ceramic tile of the Spanish peninsula, the roof tiles of the Orient, the ceramic tiles of Renaissance and post-Renaissance periods in Spain, and the tiles in use today.

Tile, as we know it, is made from a mixture of clays, flint, feldspar, and shales. The various colors, types, and surface finishes of tile are obtained by varying the ingredients and the methods of mixing and firing. Glazed and unglazed tile, which may be obtained in many different colors (see Plate IX), is used for floors and walls in bathrooms, kitchens, swimming pools, and many other areas where moisture is a problem. It is used decoratively in corridors and lobbies where soil from many hands is a problem, and it is widely used in hospitals and similar buildings where it is necessary to frequently scrub and disinfect floors and walls.

The early tile makers used local clays which were moistened and worked into shape in single pieces. Sometimes color was introduced into the body of the tile, but in some localities a colored glaze was made separately and applied to the tile as ornamentation. Crude baked tiles with painted decorations were made in the Mayan and Aztec civilizations. Blue delft tiles were made in Holland. Early Colonial settlers had tile shipped to America from Europe and faced their fireplaces with picture tiles of England and Holland.

There are two basic methods of manufacturing tile. In the "plastic method" the materials are hand molded; in the "dust-pressed" method, the excess water is removed and the almost-dry material is pressed into shape by machines. Unglazed tile obtains its colors from the ingredients used—in particular, the kinds of clays and oxides that can be added to the clays.

It was in 1876 that the first serious attempts were made to produce tile in the United States. These were crude, but nevertheless they used a one-fire process in which body and glaze were fused by firing together. Improvements continued to be made in manufacturing processes and are still being made today.

Whereas the colors of the tiles in former times were determined by local clays and materials, today raw materials are brought to the tile manufacturer from many different areas: flourlike talc from upper New York State, pyrophyllite from North Carolina and Newfoundland, china clay from Florida, flint from West Virginia, coloring substances from other distant places. One of the larger tile manufacturers prepares the materials by blending them with water, which is then removed, together with foreign matter, and the resultant finely powdered clay is then pressed into shape under great pressure. The glazed coating is automatically sprayed on in liquid form; its thickness is regulated to one-thousandth of an inch. In the firing process, the tile is very slowly passed through large kilns under intense heat. Because of the slight differences in the various materials that are used, it often happens that tiles of the same type will vary somewhat in color. The colors for each shipment are carefully selected for color consistency.

Tiles made by various companies tend to differ. It is interesting to note that for the benefit of the trade, as well as that of the consumer, the U.S. Department of Commerce has produced *A Recorded Voluntary Recommendation of the Trade* for ceramic tile floors and wall tiles. This booklet provides specifications and descriptions of the various types of tile, together with definitions of various grades—i.e., Glazed Wall Tiles, Unglazed Ceramic Mosaic Tiles, Unglazed Quarry Tiles, etc. Under the heading: Grades of Glazed Wall Tiles, Standard Grade is defined as follows:

> The tiles of this grade are as perfect as it is commercially practicable to manufacture. They are harmonious in color, although they may vary in shade. . . . They are free from biscuit cracks, ragged and shivered edges, but glazed-over biscuit chips of one-thirty-second of an inch or less are permitted. . . .

Under the title Seconds, we find:

> The tiles of this grade may have minor blemishes and defects which are not permissible in Standard Grade, but are free from blots and biscuit cracks.

Similar definitions are included for unglazed ceramic mosaic tiles and unglazed quarry tiles. There then follow recommendations for grade-marking practices and grade-mark seals and certifications of grades. At the end of the booklet, a definition is given for each adjective used in the description of the grades.

The following definitions, some of which describe color and texture, are taken from Federal Specification SS-T-308b, 11/16/59, covering ceramic tile, floor, wall, and trim units:

Definitions

Tile   A ceramic surfacing unit, usually relatively thin in relation to facial area, made from clay or a mixture of clay and other ceramic materials, called the body of

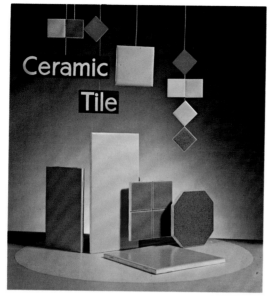

a. Ceramic

b. Crystalline

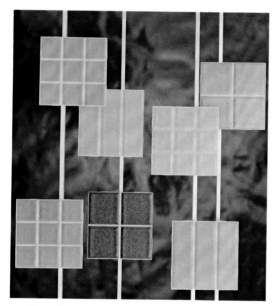

c. Scored

d. Quarry

American Olean Tile Co., Lansdale, Pa.

IX.   Types of Tile

A. Scenic Wallpaper   Courtesy of Louis W. Bowen

X. A. Wallpaper.

B. Area Rugs.

B1. Daisy Belle

B2. Stonehenge

B3. Ring Dance

(Area Rugs) Bigelow-Sanford, Inc., New York. Settings by Tom Woods, A.I.D.

the tile, having either a glazed or unglazed face and fired above red heat in the course of manufacture to a temperature sufficiently high to produce specific physical properties and characteristics.

Unglazed Tile   A hard, dense tile of homogeneous composition throughout, deriving color and texture from the materials of which the body is made. The colors and characteristics of the tile are determined by the materials used in the body, the method of manufacture, and the thermal treatment.

Glazed Tile   Glazed tile has a fused impervious facial finish composed of ceramic materials, fused onto the body of the tile which may be a nonvitreous, semivitreous, vitreous or impervious body. The glazed surface may be clear, white or colored.

Trim Units   Trim units are variously shaped units consisting of such items as bases, caps, corners, moldings, angles, etc. necessary or desirable to make a complete installation and to achieve sanitary purposes as well as architectural design for all types of tile work.

Ceramic Mosaic   Tile formed by either the dust-pressed or plastic method, usually 1/4 to 3/8 inch thick, and having a facial area of less than 6 square inches and which is usually mounted on sheets approximately 2 by 1 feet to facilitate setting. Ceramic mosaics may be of either porcelain or natural clay composition and may be either plain or with an abrasive mixture throughout.

Pavers   Unglazed porcelain or natural clay tile formed by the dust-pressed method and similar to ceramic mosaics in composition and physical properties but relatively thicker and with 6 or more square inches of facial area.

Porcelain Tile   A ceramic mosaic or paver that is generally made by the dust-pressed method of a composition resulting in a tile that is dense, fine grained, and smooth with sharply formed face, usually impervious. Colors of porcelain tile are usually of a clear luminous type, or granular blend thereof.

Natural Clay Tile   A tile made by either the dust-pressed method or the plastic method, from clays that produce a dense body having a distinctive, slightly textured appearance.

Quarry Tile   Unglazed tile, usually 6 or more square inches in surface area and 1/2 to 3/4 inch in thickness, made by the extrusion process from natural clay or shales.

Faience Tile   Glazed or unglazed tile, generally made by the plastic process, showing characteristic variations in the face, edges and glaze that give a hand crafted, nonmechanical, decorative effect.

Faience Mosaics   Faience tile that is less than 6 square inches in facial area, usually 5/16 to 3/8 inch thick, and usually mounted to facilitate installation.

Special-Purpose Tile   A tile, either glazed or unglazed, made to meet or to have specific physical design or appearance characteristics such as size, thickness, shape, color or decoration, keys or lugs on backs or sides, special resistance to staining, frost, alkalies, acids, thermal shock, physical impact, high coefficient of friction or electrical properties.

Glazed Interior Tile   A glazed tile with a body that is suitable for interior use and which is usually nonvitreous, and is not required or expected to withstand excessive impact or be subject to freezing and thawing conditions.

Glazed Tile, Extra-duty Glaze   Tile with a durable glaze that is suitable for light-duty floors and all other surfaces on interiors where there is no excessive abrasion or impact.

Glazed Ceramic Mosaics   Ceramic mosaics with glazed faces.

Ship and Galley Tile   A special quarry tile having an indented pattern on the face of the tile to produce an antislip effect.

Packing House Tile   Similar to quarry tile but usually of greater thickness.

Conductive Tile   Tile made from special body compositions or by methods that result in specific properties of electrical conductivity while retaining other normal physical properties of tile.

Impervious Tile   Tile with water absorption of 0.5 percent or less shall be classified impervious.

Vitreous   Tile with water absorption of 0.5 percent to 3 percent shall be classified vitreous.

Semivitreous   Tile with water absorption of 3 percent to 7 percent shall be classified semivitreous.

Nonvitreous   Tile with water absorption over 7 percent shall be classified nonvitreous.

The various companies make available to architects and professional interior designers color samples of various floor and wall tiles. Here is the line of one domestic producer, the American Olean Tile Company:

Ceramic Wall Tile

Bright colors	*Matte glaze colors*
Mist Green	Gardenia
Willow Green	Forest Green
Spring Green	Sage Gray
Sylvan Green	Bayberry
Pine Green	Leaf Green
Aqua Mist	Fern Green
Robins Egg	Spruce Green
Turquoise	Lobelia
Bluet	Flax Blue
Brite White	Smoke Gray
Pastel Blue	Dawn Gray
Cornflower	Antique White
Pearl Gray	Daffodil
Oyster Gray	Jonquil
Ivory	Cream
Buttercup	Parchment
Tan Tint	Vellum
Maize	Peach
Buckwheat	Honeysuckle
Suntan	Hibiscus
Tan Glo	Hydrangea
Nutmeg	
Corallin Pink	
Salmon Pink	
Berry Brown	
Spice Brown	
Sandalwood	
Pink Blush	
Coral	
Clover Red	
Lilac	
Orchid	
Gloss Black	
Gold Mist	
Salt and Pepper	

The foregoing wall-tile colors are available in the following sizes:

Glazed Interior Tile: 8 1/2 × 4 1/4 inches
                        6 × 4 1/4 inches
                        6 × 6 inches
                        4 1/4 × 4 1/4 inches
                        3 × 3 inches
                        1 3/8 × 1 3/8 inches Tile Gems*
                        4 1/4 inches Octagon
                        4 1/4 inches Scored Tile

Glazed Frostproof Tile: 4 1/4 × 4 1/4 inches
                        3 × 3 inches
                        1 3/8 × 1 3/8 inches Tile Gems* 5/16 inches thick

All sizes are cushion (rounded) edge except 4 1/4-inch Octagon, 4 1/4-inch Scored Tile, and 1 3/8 inch squares, which are square edge.

Large Size Glazed Tile: 8 1/2 × 4 1/4 inches
                        6 × 6 inches
                        6 × 4 1/4 inches

* Registered trademark, American Olean Tile Co.

Crystalline Tile
(For walls and residential floors)

Crystalline White		Crystalline Charcoal	
"	Salt and Pepper	"	Mint
"	Antique White	"	Suntan
"	Cream	"	Beige
"	Yellow	"	Mocha
"	Gray	"	Pink
"	Sage	"	Sky Blue
"	Gold Mist	"	Cornflower
"	Buckwheat	"	Cobalt
		"	Lagoon

These tiles are available in sizes 4 1/4 by 4 1/4 inches, 4 1/4-inch Octagon, 3 by 3 inches, 1 3/8 by 1 3/8 inches, and 4 1/4-inch scored tile. All are 5/16 inch thick. Sizes are square edge except the 3 by 3-inch, which is cushion edge.

Scored tile is available in one size (4 1/4 by 4 1/4 inches) and three patterns in the foregoing glazed and crystalline colors. (A scored tile is one that has been grooved to look like several smaller tiles.)

Clear, Unglazed Floor Tile
(Impervious ceramic mosaics for interior and exterior use; can be used for walls. Sizes: 1 × 1, 2 × 1, and 2 × 2 in.)

Buckskin*	Beryl*
Adobe	Petal Pink*
Teal*	Apricot
Ecru	Amber
Citron	Emerald*
Aqua*	Sapphire*
Cerulean*	Rouge
Cameo	Cinnabar*
Beige*	Sepia
Topaz*	Jade*
Celadon*	Cobalt*
Lavender	Dove Gray*
Ebony*	Pepper White*
Dawn Gray*	White*

* Available in abrasive nonslip tile.

Textured, Unglazed Floor Tile
(Impervious ceramic mosaics; can be used for walls.
Sizes: 1 × 1, 2 × 1, and 2 × 2 in.)

Palm Green*	Cocoa Brown*
Sea Green*	Reef Brown*
Surf Green	Driftwood*
Haze*	Beach Tan*
Smoke*	Doubloon
Horizon*	Copper
Lagoon Blue*	Corallin
Wine	

* Available in abrasive nonslip tile.

Accent Colors
(For contrast)

High-key bright glaze colors (Size: 1 3/8 × 1 3/8 × 5/16 in.; also custom-scored)	*High-key square ceramic mosaics*—frostproof (Size: 1 × 1 in.)
Lemon Yellow	Lemon Yellow
Violet	Violet
Regal Blue	Regal Blue
Meadow Green	Meadow Green
Gold	Gold
Platinum	Platinum
Tangerine	Tangerine
Vermilion	Vermilion
Cherry Red	Cherry Red
Bright Blue	Bright Blue

* For use with ceramic colors in chart listing Clear, Unglazed Floor Tile.

Quarry Tile

Golden Glow	Canyon Red
Fawn Gray	Sahara Starlight Abrasive
Sahara	Canyon Red Abrasive
Ember Flash	Sand Flash
Fawn Gray Starlite Abrasive	

These quarry tiles are available in the following sizes:

6 × 2 3/4 × 1/2 in.:	Sahara
	Canyon Red
4 × 4 × 1/2 in.:	Sahara
	Canyon Red
2 3/4 × 2 3/4 × 1/2 in.:	Sahara
	Canyon Red
3 7/8 × 8 × 1/2 in.:	Sahara
	Sand Flash
	Canyon Red
	Ember Flash
	Fawn Gray
6 × 6 × 3/4 in.:	Canyon Red
9 × 9 × 3/4 in.:	Sahara
	Canyon Red

Special surfaces are also available in the following sizes and colors:

Abrasive:	6 × 6 × 1/2 in.—All colors
	6 × 6 × 3/4 in.—Canyon Red
Starlite Abrasive:	6 × 6 × 1/2 in.—Canyon Red, Sahara, and Fawn Gray
Diamond Grid:	6 × 6 × 3/4 in.—Canyon Red, Sahara

Decorated Tile More than seventy decorated tile designs in size 4 1/4 by 4 1/4 inches are available to the architect or interior designer. The designs include sea life, seashells, vegetables, decanters, grain, animals, and geometric forms. Colors harmonize with glazed tile colors and are available in many color combinations. These tiles may be spotted at random in a solid-color wall, grouped in patterns, or combined with undecorated tile on an important wall.

In addition to the above, a number of handcrafted tiles are available in various colors and patterns. Like all handcrafted materials, they are artistically handsome *because of* their imperfections.

As the foregoing describes, tile is available in so many different colors and shapes that it is possible for the architect or interior designer to use the available "alphabet" in many ways. Anyone can use a single-colored tile, but it takes a skilled and practiced professional to combine tile colors and sizes to accentuate the good points of architectural spaces. If such a space is very high, horizontal patterns will be called for, but if the space has a low ceiling, vertical stripes or other patterns will help to "raise" it. In rooms with a moderately large floor surface, suggested standard patterns in various color combinations are offered by manufacturers. The choice of floor and wall tiles will depend upon the size of the room, the directional effect that the architect or designer wishes to obtain and, of course, the colors that are required.

Murals can also be created, and the colors of the tiles must be selected by the principles described in Chapter 2 on color theory. Colors must be integrated with other colors in the area; the mural designer will usually cooperate with the architect and interior designer in achieving the desired effect.

FLOORING

Carpets and Rugs

Carpets seem to have originated in the Orient; traders probably introduced them to Europe. Their magnificence was such that they were often hung as wall decorations. Carpet designs varied according to the locality in which they were made. It has been suggested that patterns containing flowers, trees, and animals[1] reflected the importance of these items in the mind of the Oriental and that he enjoyed surrounding himself with them.

While in some places animals were used in the design, in others human figures were occasionally portrayed. But basically one finds symbols which are expressions of the spiritual[2] world. In addition to symbolism in design, a complete and elaborate color symbolism was used. One's rank and status partially determined the design of his carpet: a carpet made for a prince was different from one made for a person of lesser importance. Colors varied from country to country and from tribe to tribe. Green might be the sacred color of Mohammed and, therefore, be used for prayers. In another country, blue might symbolize power. Many plants were symbolically important. One finds that the various seasons were represented by specific flowers, and the tree of life seems to have been present in almost every oriental carpet. Animals and insects were important too in the symbolic scheme of things. The butterfly signified longevity, the scarab, royal power in India. Geometrical figures of significance going back thousands of years include the triangle, the meander pattern, and the

[1] *Ciba Review,* Vols. Nos. 1–24, p. 517, September, 1937–August, 1939.
[2] *Ibid.,* p. 525.

FIG. 5.8 Carpet construction

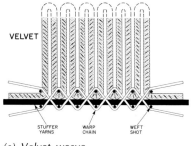

(a) Velvet weave

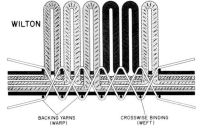

(b) Wilton weave

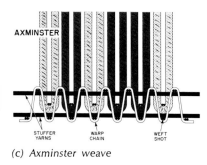

(c) Axminster weave

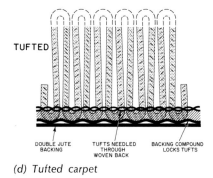

(d) Tufted carpet

Buddhist arc. Regardless of the design elements, however, a central motif is a part of almost every oriental rug. Here a person could sit or recline and survey the beauties of the design which surrounded him.

One of the characteristics of the genuine oriental rug is its thinness. When the makers of rugs in Europe and the United States tried to imitate oriental rugs, they added a backing to which the surface pile was woven.

Today, in the age of the power loom, rugs (which are used individually) and carpets (which can be sewn together) are manufactured in three different ways: woven, knitted, or tufted.

Woven Carpet   The surface pile and backing of woven carpet are interwoven at the same time, creating a single fabric. Due to the interweaving, which locks all of the yarns together in the single woven fabric, the pile yarns cannot be pulled out. Some carpet weaves presently available are velvet, wilton, and axminster. Velvet is best suited for solid-color carpet; however, tweeds, stripes, and salt-and-pepper effects can be produced on velvet looms. The usual velvet is a solid-color carpet with smooth surface and even pile. Sometimes the pile is cut to produce a plushlike surface (see Figure 5.8a). It may also be had in loop pile, or twist.

Wilton weave comes in almost unlimited numbers of textures and sculptured effects, as well as patterns. The pile is sometimes cut, sometimes left uncut; a combination of cut and uncut may also be obtained. In multicolor wiltons, one color may be seen on the surface pile, while other colors are hidden in the body of the carpet. Embossed and sculptured effects are also made by the wilton looms, and cut and uncut pile can be combined with cut pile for the top level, with loops at other levels. Another variation is to have some pile yarn straight and others twisted (see Figure 5.8b).

In the axminster weave, which is similar in appearance to handweaving, we find a complete flexibility in the use of color. In this method each tuft is inserted separately and while solid-color carpets can be made by this method, it is nearly always used for multicolored pattern carpet such as orientals, or modern and geometric designs (see Figure 5.8c).

Tufted Carpet   In the tufted process, which was only recently perfected, the tufts are attached to a previously made backing, as compared with the methods described above in which the backing and pile are integral. The tufts are held in place by a heavy coating of latex applied to the backing, which is usually cotton, jute, or kraft cord. By the use of this method, a wide variety of textures is possible. For example, the tufted pile can be made in several levels; it can be cut or uncut; and carved or striated effects can be obtained. The pile can be looped or plush. Tufted carpets are made in multicolor patterns with an increasing number of textural effects and refinements (see Figure 5.8d).

While color and pattern changes take many hours on the jacquard loom, the Colorset Process,[1] a relatively new invention, does the same thing in minutes. The process, designed for tufted carpets, permits unlimited changes in design and color. In this method, the tufted carpet is fed into a machine in spaced steps that are controlled by a series of circuits which contain the selected pattern, there being a separate circuit for each different color. The dyestuffs in this process are premetallized, and the dyestuff is drawn into the yarn and fibers all the way through to the back.

[1] E. T. Barwick Mills, Inc.

In this method, as contrasted with others, the yarn need not be changed to produce color change. As graph paper is not used in the design, "steps" and "ladders" are not necessary, and the resultant pattern is smooth and flowing. Since this method is very flexible and economical, and because the carpet can be made from any yarn (nylon, Acrilan, wool, or cotton), it is widely used.

Knitted Carpet The knitting process loops together the pile yarn, backing yarn, and stitching yarn with three sets of needles in a manner similar to knitting. Finally a coat of latex is applied on the back. Because a single-pile yarn is used for the knitting process, these carpets are usually tweeds or solid colors, and are made with cut or uncut loops either in single level or multilevel. Cut pile can be obtained by modifying the machines.

Selecting the Color Selection of the color of a carpet must be made with the realization that it will bring a great deal of color into an area and with the awareness that, generally speaking, the carpet color should be darker than the wall color because it will show less soil and will have a more comfortable reflectance value. A carpet's texture makes it appear darker than a smooth surface of the same color; therefore a carpet will seem to be darker than the color of its yarn. Generally speaking, contrasting schemes obtained by making the carpet a complement of the wall color produce a too sharp effect, and unless other factors enter into the decision, the walls and carpet should be kept in the same color family. For instance, a red carpet will be very effective in a room with pale pink walls, or a blue-green carpet can be used in a room where the draperies are blue and the chairs are green.

As might be expected, the most unusual colors are available in higher-priced lines, and less expensive carpets are available in a limited number of colors. (If carpets were available in every color and shade, the carpet dealer's range of selections would still be limited, because he would be able to stock only so many of them.) The limited range of available carpet colors sometimes makes it impossible for the experienced designer to find the more subtle colors he prefers to use. Ten years ago most color lines averaged from seven to ten colors. Today many of them have thirty-five colors or more; one line has sixty-three. As in the selection of paint, the color of a carpet, since it is to occupy so much of the space, must be selected with great care.

The color lines in a typical carpet salesroom vary according to material and manufacture. If one examines the shelves in the showroom of Stark Carpet (New York City), which sells to the trade, he may find the following carpet materials and colors:

Wool (As wool is yellowish in color, no *very* bright white, pale pink, or pale yellow carpet can be made of it)

Yellow white	Light yellow
Pale gray	Lemon yellow
Medium gray	Yellow green
Gray green	Orange green
Light blue	Avocado
Pale gray blue	Blue green
Orange	Scarlet
Pale orange	Deep red
Pumpkin	Taupe
Terra-cotta	Lavender
Pink	Brown
Orange red	

Cotton (can be made in any color since the raw material is white)

White	Deep pink
Gray	Taupe
Golden yellow	Purple
Pale yellow	Blue
Pale yellow green	Blue green
Gray orange	Green
Orange	Cocoa brown
Emerald green	Bronze

Rayon and Acetate (has a luster)

Lilac
Orange and yellow-gold blend
Red
Avocado
Stripes: gold, brown, beige, etc.

Nylon (does not look like wool; has a luster, colors are vibrant)

Bright yellow
Mustard
French ultramarine blue
Cherry red
Purple
 (in addition to standard colors)

Acrilan (has woollike appearance)

Brilliant orange	Medium blue
Brilliant red	Dark blue
Orange red	Green
Gold	Avocado
Gray gold	Taupe
Sky blue	

In addition to the foregoing, various blends of wool and nylon, Acrilan acrylic and modacrylic, and Acrilan acrylic and Verel modacrylic are available in all of the variations noted previously.

Many suppliers will dye carpets to special order, and while this practice is common, it should not be entered into lightly because of the high cost.

Area rugs, unlike carpet, do not cover the entire floor. They may be plain or patterned (see Plate X-B), and it may be said that any rug is suitable for any room if its color has been given proper consideration when planning the entire color scheme. Whereas broadloom carpet laid wall to wall is usually considered a background, rugs very often act as a focal point. Interestingly enough, most rugs that are sold by the better suppliers are monochromatic. In previous times, such as that of Louis XIV, rugs were sold only to the nobility. But the demand for them became so great that they were soon sold to all who could pay for them in order to help support the extravagances of the court.

With a rich background of design and color at hand, the modern rug designer often styles a contemporary version of Savonnerie or Aubusson or other traditional styles. Some of these are developed in as many as six color combinations. Using his own colors, the designer of today makes his rugs adaptable to contemporary usage. They are often designed to order and are usually created as follows:

1. The architect or interior designer selects a pattern.

2. The colors are selected in accordance with the color scheme. (Earth colors are often used in contemporary rugs.)

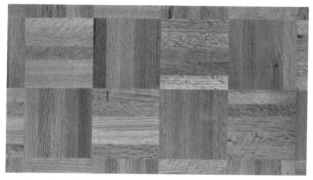

a. *Bondwood Parquet—Par (Select) red oak*

b. *Bondwood Basket Weave—Par (Select) and Better Angelique (Guiana teak)*

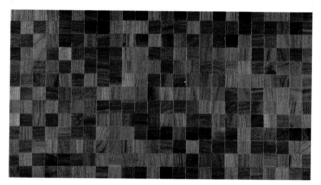

c. *Bondwood Domino—Eagle (Premium) Walnut*

d. *Bondwood Continental—Eagle (Premium) Red Oak*

e. *Bondwood Herringbone—Eagle (Premium) Red Oak*

f. *Bondwood Zigzag—Eagle (Premium) Walnut and Maple*

Harris Manufacturing Co., Johnson City, Tenn.

XI. Patterns of Wood Flooring

A.

XII.   A.   Traditional Living Room.   B.   Art Collector's Apartment.

B.

(A)   Greeff Fabrics, Inc., New York, N.Y.   (American Legacy Collection)

(B)   Du Pont Textile Fibers. Designed by D. E. Zaid, A.I.D., and John Ford, A.I.D.

3. The manufacturer makes a full-scale rendering showing the relationship of colors in the pattern.

4. The client and designer are shown the rendering, and they select the yarns.

5. A strike-off two feet square is made by the manufacturer.

6. When the strike-off is approved, all of the above items are sent to the factory and the rug is completed.

Modern rugs have the beauty of tapestries, and entire color schemes can be built around such a rug. Frequently their color and pattern are an integral part of the total design of the area.

Both the manufacturer and the client are responsible for tastes in colors. In spite of this, certain colors, such as french putty, which is neutral and beautiful, a bright cherry red (especially lovely on stairways), and a mousy-tapue seem to be perennially popular. A beautifully proportioned and designed neutral rug of warm gray or gray-brown, with a small amount of cerulean blue, seems always to be popular.

Resilient Flooring

Asphalt Tile   This product is made of mineral pigments and asbestos fibers which are mixed with a binder containing resin. One of the least expensive of the several kinds of resilient flooring, it is made in 9 by 9 inch and 12 by 12 inch tiles. It is not among the most pliable materials; therefore, it should be used only on a level, smooth bed. While it is excellent for most inexpensive installations, ordinary asphalt tile disintegrates when in contact with gasoline, solvent wax cleaners, oils, and grease. When these materials are to be present, a special greaseproof tile is recommended.

The color lines of asphalt tile vary, of course, according to the manufacturer. Certain basic similarities in color and pattern exist in asphalt and vinyl asbestos tile, and a Color Comparison Chart is issued yearly by the Asphalt and Vinyl Asbestos Tile Institute. Color comparisons are given for the products of such companies as Amtico, Armstrong, Azrock, Congoleum Nairn, Flintkote, Johns Manville, Kentile, and Ruberoid. A typical line includes the following:

Marbleized

Medium gray with sparse black veining
Dark gray with white and black veining
Light gray with sparse green veining
Medium tan with reddish-brown veining
Dark tan with white veining
Pinkish brown with white veining
Pinkish brown with white and brown veining
Pinkish brown with white, pink, and yellow veining
Medium red with white and orange veining
Dark brown with cream and orange veining
Dark brown with cream and red veining
Medium blue green with white veining
Medium blue green with white and black veining
Dark green with white veining
Olive green with white veining
Black with white veining
Black with green veining

Woodgrain
Tan with brown graining
Dark tan with cream graining
Gray tan with raised grain pattern

Gravel
Light gray gravel in a medium gray-brown bed
Light pinkish-brown gravel in a medium tan-brown bed
Medium pinkish-brown gravel in a medium tan-brown bed

Flagstone (rough surface)
Dark gray with pale buff striations
Medium gray green with red striations
Medium reddish brown with darker red striations
Dark brown

Cork
Imitation ground cork spot pattern in several shades of light tan and dark
tan on a medium tan background

Stone
Pale pink on a pinkish gray background
Pale tan on darker tan background
Dark yellow gray on darker tan background
Light yellow gray on darker tan background
Light greenish gray on darker greenish gray background

Terrazzo
Light gray and pink on medium gray background
Light warm gray and pale orange on dark gray background

Carnival
Metallic flecks (gold, silver, bronze) on medium warm-gray background
Gold flecks on light cool-gray background

Vinyl Asbestos Tile   This product, made of vinyl resins and asbestos fibers, is available, according to the patterns used, in thicknesses of 1/16, 3/32, and 1/8 inch and in sizes 9 by 9 inches and 12 by 12 inches. More expensive than asphalt tile, it is more resistant to grease and is made in a large number of subtle but rich colors and patterns.

In one line, marbleized patterns are available in six shades of blue gray, four shades of green gray, one in warm gray with brown veining, two in green, six in shades of tan, and seven in brown. For the most part, the veining is of the same color as the tile, but is lighter or darker.

Another line includes tiles with a stone-chip appearance that is available in six shades of warm gray, three shades of pinkish gray, one in warm gray with blue "chips," one in pale brown, one in gray green, two in shades of "cork" and white, three in "cork," one in light blue gray with sparse gold veining, two in pale gray with flecks of gold, blue, and pink, and one in warm gray with flecks of gold, bronze, and silver.

A third line includes imitation travertine in one shade of white, three shades of warm gray, one of deep olive green, and one of brick red. In addition, this line includes a marble-chip design in shades of warm gray and pinkish gray.

A fourth line includes plain tiles in strong shades of golden yellow, orange, red, bright blue, yellow green, deep olive green, light gray, light brown, deep brown, and black. Still another pattern is available in a pebble design (see Figure 5.9) in beige, white, tan, and ivory. Feature strips, available in 1-inch widths, may be had in these

FIG. 5.9 *Vinyl asbestos tile, Excelon Pebblette design*

solid colors to produce special designs, and insets of special motifs are also available.

Rubber Tile This is a durable, waterproof, and relatively noiseless material. It is made in plain or marbleized designs in 6 by 6-inch 9 by 9-inch, and 12 by 12-inch squares and 18 by 36-inch rectangles, in thicknesses of 3/32, 3/16, and 1/8 inch. A typical marbleized color line includes:

Light beige with black veining
Medium beige with yellow and brown veining
Warm gray with red and green veining
Gray brown with pink and black veining
Medium brown with deeper brown and white veining
Bluish gray with black and white veining
Golden yellow with brown and white veining
Terra-cotta with white veining
Pink with yellow veining
Blue green with white veining
Green with white veining
Olive green with white veining
Black with white veining

Vinyl Sheet Flooring This material is expensive, because its wearing surface is made for the most part of vinyl resin compounds. It makes a resilient floor that is highly resistant to grease, alkalis, and wear. Depending on the manufacturer, its thickness may be 0.090, 0.070, 0.065 inch, etc.

Because it can be manufactured in a wide range of colors and patterns, and because the joints are few (the sheets are 6 feet wide and up to 80 feet in length), it is an ideal material for the architect and interior designer. Pattern is limited only by the imagination of the designer and the requirements of the job at hand.

Patterns include tessera (see Figure 5.10), small pieces of "marble" set in a darker background, and slate, brick, wood parquet, chip, terrazzo, and plain. A color sampling follows:

Tessera
White chips in gray background
Pinkish-white and yellow chips in gray background
Buff and pink chips in brown background
Green chips in darker green background
Gold and black chips in brown background
Pale-golden chips in dark yellow background
Blue-green chips in green background
Pale-blue chips in darker pale-blue background
Pinkish-gray chips in gray background
Pink, blue, and white chips in gray background
Blue and green chips in dark green background
Gray and blue chips in dark blue background
Pink, blue, and yellow chips in gray background
Yellow and orange chips in gray background

Slate and brick
Rectangular pieces of brick-red slate with dark gray joints
Red bricks in pattern with light gray joints
White bricks in pattern with light gray joints
Slate gray rectangular pieces of slate with light gray joints

Wood parquet
Light wood tone with medium brown joints
Dark wood tone with dark brown joints

FIG. 5.10   Sheet vinyl—Corlon tessera design with custom insets

Chip
   Light gray
   Dark gray
   Gray green
   Light beige
   Medium beige
   Dark beige

Terrazzo
   Warm- and cool-gray chips on gray background
   Light and dark green chips on green background
   White and gold chips on gray background
   Buff, pink, and gray with gold chips on brown background

Plain colors

White	Turquoise
Gray beige	Spectrum blue
Deep brown wood tone	Purple
Umber	Spectrum red
Black	Orange
Yellow green	

Vinyl Tile   Vinyl tile is usually made in 9 by 9 inch and 12 by 12 inch tiles. Its patterns, according to the make, include solid colors, terrazzo, travertine, translucent, marble, broken marble stone patterns, and mosaics. The designs are inspired by real, but expensive, materials.

Solid colors include:

Butter yellow	Yellow green
Orange	Tan
Bright red	Light gray
Larkspur blue	Dark gray
Spectrum blue	Brown
Green	Terra-cotta

Terrazzo colors include:
   White with black, brown, or green flecks
   Light, medium, and dark gray
   Spectrum yellow with brown and white flecks
   Butter yellow with brown and white flecks
   Tan brown with brown and white flecks
   Terra-cotta with brown and cream flecks
   Powder blue with white flecks
   Dark green with white flecks
   Black with white flecks

Travertine colors include:

White	Terra-cotta
Beige	Pale taupe
Pink	Olive green
Peach	Warm gray
Gray beige	

Marble
   White with gray veining
   Pale pink with medium pink veining
   Medium pink with tan veining
   Greenish white with green veining
   Peach with darker peach veining
   Black with white veining

Broken marble
   Pale pink with white veining
   Peach with deeper peach veining
   White
   Green with white veining
   Medium pink with white veining
   Black with white veining

Stone patterns
   White with gold joints between stones
   White with blue joints between stones
   White with taupe joints between stones
   White with green joints between stones
   Tan with darker tan joints
   Black with tan joints
   Blue with gray-blue joints
   Terra-cotta with gray joints

Embossed grainings
   Tan
   Gray orange
   Orange
   Brown

Mosaic
   Tan and white "tiles"
   Yellow and white "tiles"
   Beige brown "tiles"
   Orange brown "tiles"
   Yellow, green, and white "tiles"
   Blue and green "tiles"

As one may gather from the above, the resilient flooring designs available today are taken, for the most part, from expensive materials that many people cannot afford to use. Patterns and combinations, particularly in vinyl tiles, are almost limitless in number, and colors are so true that it is almost impossible to tell the real material from the imitation. Custom patterns, while they are usually more expensive, permit the imaginative designer to combine color and scale in almost any way that he wishes. A field of beige stone-patterned "tiles" may be broken into squares by the use of "walnut" strips (see Figure 5.11). "Brick" may be laid in any patterns, or in groups of four which are separated by dark "wood" strips. Traditional marble patterns may be imitated with great fidelity by the use of stock "marbles," both light and dark (see Figure 5.12), or contemporary designs can be developed. Floors of "wooden planks" in random sizes, complete with "pegs" and color variations, may be had, as may "delft" tile floors (see Figure 5.13), divided by plain colored strips. And so on. One needs only imagination and an adequate budget.

Cork Flooring   A comfortable and beautiful floor can be obtained by the use of cork tile flooring. Since cork is a natural material, and since it is ground and mixed with a binder before it is pressed into shape, a fair amount of color variation can be expected. These colors will range from a medium gray orange to a gray brown. Because of the process of manufacture, it is also possible to obtain a great many different effects. For instance, a pattern may contain alternate strips of light, finely ground cork and darker, coarser cork. Like those of wood, the colors in which cork is available are relatively neutral; almost any color may be used with it. Furthermore, the cork enhances the colors. In addition to its use as a flooring material, cork may be used as a finish for walls (see Plate XII-B).

FIG. 5.11 Vinyl tile—Promenade design

Terrazzo This material (see Figure 5.14) makes one of the most durable, soil- and water-resistant floors known. It is usually applied over a 2-inch layer of stone concrete, and consists of a 1-inch layer made up of cement, marble chips, and sand (and sometimes abrasives) applied almost dry. When it is in place, it is rolled and worked into the concrete bed. When it has thoroughly set, it is honed and polished by machines made for this purpose.

There are two basic kinds of terrazzo patterns: those made with gray cement, and those made with white cement. Pictures of the various color patterns may be seen in the *Catalogue and Design Book* furnished by The National Terrazzo & Mosaic Association, Inc. Each plate is given a number, and the desired pattern is ordered by that number. Although the color reproduction is very accurate, it is well to ask the contractor for a sample of the terrazzo you have specified. Nothing takes the place of the actual material for fidelity of color and pattern. In selecting varicolored terrazzo floors, it should be remembered that the result, i.e., what one sees when the material has been installed and finished, is an average of all of the colors used.

Descriptions of some of the most attractive plates follow:

Gray portland cement terrazzo plates

#101	White chips in a gray bed
102	White chips with a sprinkling of dark green chips in a gray bed
103	White chips with a sprinkling of yellow, black, and brown chips in a gray bed
104	White chips with a sprinkling of black chips in a gray bed
105	White chips with a sprinkling of yellow, green, and brown chips in a gray bed
106	White chips with a sprinkling of black chips in a gray bed
107	Cream chips in a bed of gray cement
108	White and green chips in a bed of gray cement
109	Pink chips in a bed of gray cement
110	White chips in a bed of terra-cotta cement
112	White, red, green chips in a bed of gray cement
113	White and yellow chips in a bed of gray-yellow cement
118	Brown and yellow chips in a bed of light brown cement
124	Pale pink, brown and black in gray cement
133	Yellow and several shades of green in gray cement
136	Black and reddish brown chips in gray cement
140	Black and white chips (mostly black) in a dark gray bed
142	Black chips in a dark gray bed

The following plates are, generally speaking, lighter and brighter in color and produce pastel shades. A general overview of white cement plates shows floors that produce an average of warm gray, peach, pink, brown, dark yellow, mauve tones, green, both light and dark.

White portland cement terrazzo plates

#202	White and gray chips in an off-white ground
206	Light and dark brown chips in an off-white ground
233	Burgundy with a sprinkling of white in a dark green ground
241	Black and gold in a white bed

When terrazzo is used in large spaces, the sizes of the chips should be increased. This type of floor originated with the Venetians and is extremely attractive. In Vene-

FIG. 5.12   *Vinyl tile—onyx design*

FIG. 5.13   *Vinyl tile—delft design*

tian terrazzo, large, medium, and small chips of marble are used, but the large chips, some of which are as much as 1 3/4 inches long, predominate. The additional cost of installing this type of floor is well repaid in the dramatic results obtained.

Venetian terrazzo plates
- #300 White and pale gray yellow in a gray ground
- 301 Levanto—deep red and deep green with a small amount of white in a pale-brown ground
- 302 Large dark green chips and small medium green chips in a gray-green ground
- 303 Black and white chips in a charcoal-gray ground

In all terrazzo work it is necessary to provide dividers to control and localize setting shrinkage and to localize flexure cracks when they occur. Dividers may be of half-hard brass, white metal (zinc alloy), or plastic and composition made in various colors.

Terrazzo Tiles Whereas terrazzo as such is poured and ground in place, a similar material made in precast tiles is available in sizes 12 by 12 by 1 inches, weighing approximately 10 pounds per square foot, and 16 by 16 by 1 1/8 inches weighing approximately 13 pounds per square foot. The finish is factory-honed, and the tiles arrive at the job ready to be set in desired patterns. Generally speaking, the colors and materials used resemble those of the traditional type of terrazzo.

Wall Terrazzo Terrazzo can, of course, be used for walls as well as floors. In addition, prefinished wall tiles available in size 12 by 12 by 1 1/8 inches may be obtained in many different textures and colors. In these tiles, the chips of highly polished marble project from the lowered matrix, and the natural variations in value and color provide an extremely rich appearance. The joints may be light or dark according to the designer's wishes.

Epoxy Tile Resilient epoxy tile as manufactured by, say, Terrafino Company is available where a hard-surface, grease-resistant flooring is desired. It is available in many terrazzolike combinations, including:

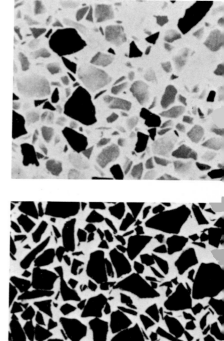

FIG. 5.14 Terrazzo

Beige and brown in an off-white background
Blue gray and black in an off-white background
Light and dark green in an off-white background
Black in a medium gray background
White and peach in a dark gray background
Black and burgundy in an off-white background

Wood

There are four basic types of wood flooring: plank, strip, parquet, and fabricated wood blocks. All of these may be had in walnut, beech, birch, oak, both red and white, and maple.

Strip flooring is of two types—unfinished for sanding and finishing after it is installed—Sizes: 25/32 by 2 1/4, 25/32 by 1 1/2, 1/2 by 2, and 3/8 by 1 1/2 inches; and prefinished—Sizes: 25/32 by 3 1/4, 25/32 by 2 1/4, and 1/2 by 2 inches. Plank flooring is 3 to 8 inches wide. Parquet flooring is made in 1-, 1 1/2-, or 2-inch widths which are 5/16 inch thick, as well as in 2 1/4-inch widths which are 13/16 inch thick. Wood blocks vary in width from 2 1/4 to 4 inches. Fabricated wood blocks are made in squares from 6 3/4 to 11 3/4 inches and in rectangles about 6 by 12 inches.

BondWood Parquet—Par (Select) Red Oak

BondWood Basket Weave—Par and Better Angelique (Guiana Teak)

BondWood Domino—Eagle (Premium) Walnut

BondWood Continental—Eagle (Premium) Red Oak

BondWood Herringbone—Eagle (Premium) Red Oak

BondWood Zigzag—Eagle (Premium) Walnut and Maple

FIG. 5.15 Wood flooring patterns

The beauty of wood flooring (see Figure 5.15) is not only in the colors that are available but also in the variation of color and pattern which the natural product supplies. The finishing of wood flooring at the job will depend upon the kind of wood. Since the cellular structure of wood varies according to species, the finishing process will depend upon the material at hand. For a clear finish, a sealer—which will penetrate the wood and actually enter the pores—should be used; it adds strength and hardness to the surface. Floors which do not require filler may be finished by the application of stain (usually used for oak floors), after which the floor should be sanded. Next a thin coat of shellac is applied. The floor is then given another sanding, a second coat of shellac, and a final sanding. A coat of paste wax, which should be applied about fifteen hours later, will supply a polish.

Light-colored floors may be finished as follows: Wood filler should be rubbed into the grain and rubbed off after about twenty minutes, a thin coat of white shellac applied, and the floor sanded. A final coat of floor varnish thinned with turpentine should then be applied. The color of the finished floor will, of course, depend upon the color of the wood that is used.

Prefinished wood flooring is obtainable in pale yellowish ash, light oak, maple, medium shades, such as cherry, and deeper tones, such as mahogany or cedar. Laminated oak strip, plank, or block floors may be obtained in a golden yellow or deeper brown. In addition, more expensive floors in teak or walnut are available and these may be used singly or in combinations of light and dark wood to form a basket weave or other patterns (see Plate XI).

CEILINGS

Plaster ceilings may, of course, be painted any color. For example, they may be painted a pale tone of the adjoining wall color, or perhaps a dark tone if they are unusually high or if there are pipes which cannot otherwise be masked. Wallpaper applied on a high ceiling is often very effective, but this technique must be studied carefully to avoid a closed-in or heavy feeling. Wallpaper is also useful in rooms with slanted ceilings or dormers to give the room unity.

Ceilings which are treated acoustically are a different matter, however. Although the temptation to paint acoustic tile is always present, the paint severely reduces the acoustic quality and will often reduce it to the point where the tile must be replaced. Acoustic material is divided into two categories:

1. That in which the acoustic material is formed into squares or rectangles and applied directly to the ceiling

2. That in which the acoustic material is placed inside perforated metal pans

Acoustic material, usually warm white in color, is patterned in various ways—to imitate travertine, for example, or notched with holes formed by the pattern to collect the noise and dissipate it. Tiles 12 inches square are usually used when the material is applied directly to the ceiling, but larger sizes are used when in suspended ceilings. Metal pans, hung from the structural ceiling, form the obvious ceiling finish and the acoustic material is placed in these pans. This type of installation is particularly advantageous in situations where moisture or maintenance are serious problems, for example in food-preparation areas where hygiene is to be considered. Such ceilings will often incorporate heating, air conditioning, and lighting systems. The metal pans can be obtained in standard painted finishes, stainless steel, or custom colors. There are numerous variations for installation of this type of acoustic material.

Where noise is a great problem, it is sometimes advisable to combine utility and beauty by fastening colored carpet material to the ceiling.

Translucent ceiling systems consisting of sheets of glass or plastic material which diffuse the light emitted from bulbs or tubes between the translucent ceiling and the structural ceiling above provide dramatic effects. The color given off by such a ceiling will, of course, depend upon the color of the lighting used and the type of diffuser used; this must be given careful study (see Chapter 3, The Effects of Light on Color).

Some ceiling systems are constructed so that they have the appearance of a series of coffers. In this type of ceiling, light is provided at the top of some or all of the coffers, and the lighting source is, therefore, obscured. Such ceiling coffers are sometimes alternated with flat areas of acoustic material; variations in color and tone are thereby obtained.

chapter six

THE
APPLICATION OF
COLOR: FURNITURE

THE design and construction of furniture is probably one of the oldest arts. In ancient Egypt, furniture of wood was inlaid with ivory and ebony, and gold ornament was often applied. Numerous pieces of furniture used by the ancient Greeks and Romans show a use of wood as well as bronze, marble, and iron. The forms were, to a great extent, architectural in character, and like many works of architecture they were sometimes carved and painted. Tables richly decorated with bronze, precious metals, and marble and frequently inlaid with wood, ivory, and mosaic were used in Pompeii. Like the Romans and the Greeks, the Pompeians dined while in a reclining position and their couches were usually decorated with colorful tapestries and cushions—the first use of upholstery.

During the Gothic period, furniture was for the most part made of wood and was heavy in proportion and detail. Again, the ornament was architecturally inspired: motifs included Gothic arches, buttresses, crockets, etc. While the furniture of ancient Egypt, Greece, and Rome was mainly designed to be used in one place, Gothic furniture was designed to be movable. Chairs, for instance, were basically chests that could be easily moved in case of political turmoil. Because of the relatively cold climate, beds were large and enclosed with a canopy and curtains. Tables and chairs were of the trestle type so that they could be dismantled and quickly moved if necessary.

During the Italian Renaissance, furniture was rich in color and, for the most part, massive. In the homes of the wealthy, at least, it was more plentiful than in earlier periods. Beds continued to be large, and were often carved and painted; tables were plain or carved, and were made in many sizes. Furniture for the display of art, such as pedestal supports for statues and ornaments, writing cabinets, and storage cabinets, as well as framed mirrors and pictures, were used—all of which reflected the artistic appreciation of the times. Hand carvings and paintings were common in establishments of the wealthy. A large group of artisans was developed for this work; some of them were later imported to France by Francis I and subsequent French rulers.

In France, the Gothic period remained in vogue for some time, and furniture was similar to that used in Italy. Under Louis XIV a guild of cabinetmakers was formed by Le Brun and directed to create new and beautiful furniture. These and later groups developed the various kinds and styles of furniture that were the precursors of modern furniture. Now the furniture became more comfortable, and it was upholstered or cushioned with the magnificent fabrics of France.

The furniture of the Early Renaissance in England was developed from the Gothic styles and those of the Italian Renaissance. At first it was heavy in character. The main pieces were wardrobes, dressers, chests, chairs, tables, stools, and beds. The wood was sometimes enriched by surface grooving, and coats of arms were used. Generally the early furniture, such as that of the Elizabethan period, was heavy in proportion. During the reign of Charles II, furniture became more comfortable, and Flemish scrollwork was popular. Now cushions and upholstery became more elaborate and brilliant in color. During the William and Mary period, wood veneer came into wide use, and great attention was given to the beauty of the graining in wood pieces. Upholstery materials of all kinds continued to be used. During the Queen Anne and Early Georgian periods, furniture became finer in detail, and the beauty of veneering and grain continued to receive great attention.

Under Sir Christopher Wren, Abraham Swan, and Batty Langley, classical architectural elements were introduced, and the curved line in structural and panel forms was gradually eliminated. Mahogany continued to be used in cabinetmaking; solid mahogany was often used instead of veneering. Chippendale furniture, which was made famous by Thomas Chippendale's *Gentleman and Cabinet Maker's Director* (1754), for the most part evinced the more refined furniture styling of the time. Designs were taken from many sources, usually made in mahogany, and Chinese-inspired designs were given the name "Chinese Chippendale."

While other books of furniture designs predated and postdated those of Chippendale, none had quite so widespread an effect. George Hepplewhite's *Cabinetmakers' and Upholsterers' Guide,* which stressed slender proportions, also stressed such surface enrichment as painting and the use of satinwood. Carved ornament was often used. In 1790, Sheraton's *Cabinet-maker and Upholsterer's Drawing Book,* which contained styles that were borrowed from many sources, was published. This book stressed the straight line and the segmental curve, and had a profound effect on the designers of England and the United States. During the Adam, or Neoclassic, period, a deliberate effort was made to unify interiors by making all elements and objects in them of a single style.

The interiors of smaller houses in the late eighteenth century were sparsely furnished, and upholstery was not often used. This austerity was carried over into the simple homes in early America. During the Regency period few new ideas appeared. The style of the French Empire period had its effect on English designs, but the simple, clean lines of the styles immediately preceding it seem not to have been popular, and styles of former periods were often used. Designers seeking new and simple designs reached back into Greek antiquity for their forms and ornaments. Simplicity, however, was soon washed away during the Victorian period by the flood of clumsily designed, ornamented, and manufactured furniture, the forms of which were badly copied from Italian, Turkish, and Greek sources as well as from the entire Gothic spectrum.

As mentioned in Chapter 1, the furniture of the early periods of the United States was influenced greatly by that of the various lands from which the individual settlers had come. For the most part, the furniture was practical and useful, much of it made of wood. Since the average household could not afford many pieces of furniture, the various items—the table chair, for instance—were made to do more than one job.

Much of the fine furniture of the Georgian period in the early eighteenth century was either imported from England or made by craftsmen who had emigrated from that land. Inspired by the work of the many cabinetmakers in England and by their cabinetmaking books, the wealthy householder sought to obtain richer furniture for his home. The Philadelphia school, craftsmen who gathered in Philadelphia between 1742 and 1796, produced many fine pieces, while a similar group in Newport, Rhode Island, including John Goddard and John Townsend, produced fine examples of the blockfront type. Similar groups sprang up in other areas.

During the Federal period (1780–1830) professional architects began to work in the United States for the first time—John McComb in New York, Thomas Jefferson in Virginia, Benjamin Latrobe in Washington, Sam McIntire in Salem, and James Hoban in South Carolina. The delicacy of their work demanded equally delicate furniture, and while the Adam influence was more apparent in interior design than in furniture, the Hepplewhite designs seemed to have been particularly popular at this time. Similarly, the graceful work of Duncan Phyfe, produced between 1790 and 1830 in New York, usually in mahogany, seems to have been often used. During the American Eagle period (1812) patriotism was symbolized in furniture and other arts by the use of the eagle. This form appeared on numerous items, including picture frames, clocks, and wall brackets.

During the American Victorian period, Gothic forms again came into prominence, and it was not until the Philadelphia Exposition of 1876 that the public was ready for finer furniture. At the end of the nineteenth century, Americans who traveled in Europe or read art periodicals which displayed antiques again became enamored of antiques and brought many to this country. This practice continues today; one often places an antique piece in an otherwise contemporary room.

CASE PIECES

The wood finishes of today's furniture depend upon availability as well as the workability of the species at hand and the personal tastes of the designer and client. Walnut seems to have retained its popularity since the Italian Renaissance. During the French Renaissance oak, walnut, and poplar were used. During the eighteenth century, interiors were rich and colorful; ebony, oak, sycamore, chestnut, wildwood, kingwood, amaranth, and fruitwoods such as apple, pear, and cherry were used in marquetry. Mahogany was widely used during the middle of the eighteenth century when

Chippendale produced his enduring designs, and Hepplewhite popularized the use of satinwood.

In the early days of colonial America, mahogany, which was then popular in England, was used not only in pieces imported from England but also in those made by English craftsmen who had come to the United States.

The finishes of early American mahogany furniture ranged in color from medium orange brown through yellow brown, gray brown, and reddish brown. These are imitated today by furniture manufacturers who specialize in reproducing pieces reminiscent of the past.

Walnut is widely used by wood-furniture manufacturers today. It varies in shade from a gray brown to a reddish brown or yellowish brown. There are a number of ways to finish walnut furniture. Oil-finish walnut has a mat appearance, while lacquer finish has a sheen. The number of woods and wood finishes that are available in today's market will vary from manufacturer to manufacturer. A casual walk through one showroom reveals that walnut, teak, ebony, cherry, maple, myrtle burl, and oak are available; some pieces are finished in black or chinese-red lacquer. In another showroom one sees three kinds of rosewood finishes, one type being brownish, another reddish brown, and the third a lacquer which has an orange appearance. This showroom's mahogany is available in dark gray brown, pinkish brown, and gray-yellow brown, and its teak varies in color from dull gray tan to gray orange to deep gray brown. It also exhibits furniture made of a scrubbed rosewood, which is a weatherbeaten light gray in quality.

Most manufacturers find it expedient to limit the number of colors and finishes. For example, one of the larger manufacturers of case pieces specializes in redwood, walnut, rosewood, teak, and oak; another limits its finishes to mat-finish teak, oiled walnut, oiled ash, and rosewood; still another offers only walnut. Some showrooms display only one kind of wood.

FIG. 6.1 Desk with rosewood top and ebony-walnut base

For commercial furniture, the manufacturers have developed finishes which will withstand heavy use. These are available in several shades of walnut, from light to

dark brown. "Executive" pieces are available in sophisticated patterns in mahogany, teak, rosewood, or ebony. For more practical use, such as in general offices, hotels, and institutions, plastic laminates which simulate the popular woods are often used.

For additional beauty and color and grain contrast, designers sometimes use several different kinds of wood, faintly reminiscent of marquetry, in one piece of furniture (see Figure 6.1). Glass, marble, travertine, and leather are often used for the tops of desks, tables, and chests (see Figure 6.2).

Metals, such as stainless steel, brushed or polished chrome, or anodized aluminum, are frequently combined with wood in the framing of chairs, tables, and cabinets.

Metal is also used in the manufacture of desks, files, chairs, beds, and tables, for commercial and institutional use. These pieces are available in a wide range of colors and finishes. A glance at a typical color card will reveal a deep beige, a pale beige, a medium gray green, and a deep gray green. Custom finishes might include an ivory, greenish bronze, deep red, french ultramarine blue, chinese red, off-white, deep brown, putty, and charcoal gray—a wide palette from which the designer may choose.

UPHOLSTERED FURNITURE

The designs of chairs and sofas evolved at a rather slow pace until the beginning of the so-called "functional" era, when it seems to have suddenly occurred to designers that furniture should be designed to fit the human anatomy. While the first attempts at functional seating design did not bring forth especially good results, there are today dozens of designs which successfully break from the past in form and construction. While wood continues to be used for the frames of much of our furniture, other materials are being used. For instance, one finds steel bases, as on Peter Hoyte's "Orbit" chair; tubular steel construction with foam-rubber cushions, as in Eva Hauser's Swedish rocker; and enamel or chrome-finish steel frames, as in Robin Cruikshank's "DC-102" dining chair. Eero Saarinen's "Tulip" chair is made of plastic and cast

FIG. 6.2 Desk with white-veined marble top and ebony-walnut base

aluminum; molded plywood is used by Charles Eames in his armchair and footstool, which have down-filled hide cushions and bases of steel and aluminum. The famous Barcelona chair, designed in 1929 for the Barcelona Exhibition by Miës van der Rohe, has a polished steel frame, hide straps, and buttoned hide-covered cushions. Other very comfortable form-fitting chairs with frames of laminated plywood include Alvar Aalto's Finnish cantilever easy chair, designed in 1935. The "Egg" chair of Arne Jacobsen employs light plastic for the frame and a covering of foam rubber.

While most of these chairs use materials which we have mentioned before, the form of each chair or sofa dictates to the designer the kind of fabric that each chair will accept. Chairs of the great contemporary designers seem to achieve a clean, architectural appearance when upholstered in black, white, olive, deep gray, or tan leather. These colors accentuate the clean sculptural quality and exquisite lines of these chairs. Smaller and more playful chair designs will often accept fabrics in colorful solids, stripes, and geometrics.

Fabrics

One of the largest and most varied sources of color available to the architect and interior designer for interior work is the field of fabrics. A sampling of the racks in a decorative-fabric showroom will make the beholder aware of the fact that there are many different kinds available; more appear every day. In the past, the words "medium-weight upholstery covering" described cotton, linen, and silk in brocades, chintz, cretonne, crewel embroidery, moire, damask, satin, sateen, and taffeta. Heavy-weight fabrics included crewel embroidery, mohair, brocatelle, damask, monk's cloth, petit point, twill, velvet velour, velveteen, and lampas. Today these fabrics are still available, but there is also a host of new fabrics, including many which are composed of man-made fibers. Many fabrics are blends of several different fibers to increase resistance to wear and often enhance their beauty. Fabrics are available in solids, mixtures, stripes, and printed designs.

It should be remembered that the colors of traditional fabrics were determined by the materials available, the technical limitations of the times, the taste of the society in which they were developed, and the light in which they were to be used. One may see in traditional fabrics a great many subtleties, nuances, and details that can only be understood and appreciated if they are properly used in today's interiors. While it is possible to use contemporary fabrics in traditional interiors (or vice versa) a great deal of experience in color is required. The interiors of a courthouse, built in, say, 1837, in which there are finely studied architectural interior details, will be complemented by damasks which are reproduced from authentic designs of the same period. There are many "restoration" fabrics on the market which reproduce the design and the colors of the several historical periods. Typically, damasks of our Colonial times are available in tan gold, cream gold, blue green, yellow green, brilliant red, and soft gray blue. The color scheme of an office done in the Colonial style might include curtains of a documentary print with a gray-beige background and a blue-green tree pattern, one chair in the same fabric, a deep red desk chair, medium green side chairs, and a beige carpet.

A bedroom in the French tradition might include a small white, pink, and slate-blue cotton print with headboard, canopy, bedspread, and upholstered chairs all done in the same fabric.

English chintzes in the traditional style are also extremely popular. One with red and deep blue flowers on a natural-white background can be used for upholstery and curtains, with perhaps a solid-colored accent in gray blue on one chair (Plate XII-A.)

Interestingly enough, many clients demand period design, style, and color, probably because they feel that it gives them a cultural link with the past. At the other end of the scale, however, an increasing number of clients are asking for, and getting, modern upholstery and curtain fabrics that are in keeping with the architecture of today. The designers of period rooms often use soft pastel blendings, while those who produce contemporary rooms achieve their aims by making bold statements in color. In a typical contemporary interior one may see a great many brilliant colors on plain, striped, or geometric-patterned fabrics, woven and printed. Stripes of narrow or varying widths might include almost primary hues such as light and dark blue, orange brown and red, red and blue, blue and green, orange and yellow, or orange and black. One may use a bright spectrum-blue sofa with a bright green chair, or a beige sofa with bright yellow and blue pillows on it. In rooms where brilliant upholstery colors are used, accessories of black, white, olive, putty, deep blue gray, purple, plum, and gray are used as counterpoints.

Contemporary fabrics offer many interesting color combinations and effects when blended: say, lemon yellow and orange, orange and green, red and black, blue and green, purple and blue, beige and white, light and dark gray, orange and burnt orange, light and dark blue, olive and cerulean blue, black and white, brown and black, fuchsia and purple, or raspberry red and black. These combinations are available in many fascinating weaves which range from very light-weight to nubby and heavy-weight fabrics.

In addition to the clearly defined traditional and contemporary upholstery fabrics, one finds fabrics which are traditionally inspired but modern in feeling (see Plate XIII). In the collection pictured, the palette has been selected so that the colors are compatible with each other. The basic cloth is available in thirty-two colors; other fabrics in the collection include a large damask-type weave, a small allover weave, a horizontal stripe, a medium-scaled hourglass weave, a classic scroll, a floral, and a vertical stripe.

Each designer designs toward a particular segment of taste, and there are many fabrics available for those who occupy a position between the extremes.

Special upholstery fabrics have been developed for use in commercial situations which require unusual wearing ability, or other special qualities such as flame resistance or soil resistance.

Textile dyeing   All fabrics were at one time colored with vegetable dyes. Today most fabrics are dyed with less expensive synthetic dyes. A partial list[1] of dyes is given below, but it must be remembered that chemists are continually inventing more brilliant and light- and washfast dyes, and new dyes for new synthetic fabrics.

Dye	Qualities	Fabrics
Vegetable extract dyes (also dyes from animals and minerals)	Limited range of colors. Expensive	All
Basic dyes (Organic base soluble in simple acid)	Not always colorfast. Give brilliant color	Hemp, linen, silk, wool; also cotton and rayon when binding agent is added

[1] *Encyclopedia of Textiles*, American Fabrics Magazine, ed., Englewood Cliffs, N.J.: Prentice-Hall, Inc., 1960, pp. 469–471.

Dye	Qualities	Fabrics
Direct dyes	More lightfast and not resistant to loss of color by washing. Less brilliant than basic dyes Wide color range*	Cotton, linen, cellulose rayon, wool, silk, nylon
Acid dyes (Napthol or azo dyes)	Produce bright, colorfast reds	Nylon, silk, wool piece-goods
Sulfur dyes	Poor resistance to sunlight. Colors not brilliant. Weakens structure of some fabrics	Cotton, linen, cellulose rayons
Vat dyes (Made from anthraquinone, carbazole, and indigo)	Very lightfast. Washfast Most durable of dyes	Cotton, linen, rayon, silk, wool, all types of fibers
Acetate dyes	Produce brilliant colors	Useful on synthetic fibers, especially nylon
Alizarin dyes (synthetically produced)	Produce bright, dark red, as well as other colors	Wool, sometimes cotton
Aniline dyes	Usually used to obtain black. Lightfast. Washfast	Cotton
Azoic dyes (from aromatic hydrocarbons)	Light fast. Wetfast	Dacron
Chrome dyes	Very light- and washfast	Woolens, worsteds
Developed dyes	Produce same shades as direct dyes, but more fade-resistant	Cotton, rayon
Neutral dyes Similar to chrome dyes, but metal salts are mixed in before use	Flat, drab colors	Wool. Synthetics such as nylon

Dyeing Processes The following processes are used on yarns:†

Process	Description	Yarn	Finished Product
Stock dyeing	Fibers are completely immersed prior to spinning or blending. Economical only for quantities in excess of 5,000 lbs.	Mixtures, blends, and unusual and rich cloths	Good color. Lightfast
Top dyeing	Thread-like fibers are combed and wound on tops, then immersed in tanks, where dye is forced through fibers	Worsted fabrics	Dyed thread suitable for blending of colors. Lightfast if dye is pre-metalized‡
Solution dyeing	Dyeing occurs while fiber material is in liquid state	Synthetic fibers	Good color. Excellent lightfastness
Yarn dyeing	Yarn is immersed in dye solution and turned to force dye through it	Any fiber in yarn form	Lightfastness can be adjusted to end use of fabric
Color space dyeing	Yarn is colored at prescribed intervals along its length	Nylon	Light- and washfast. Multicolored for random effects

* Susheela Dantyagi, *Fundamentals of Textiles and Their Care*, Bombay: Orient Longmans, Ltd., 1964.
† *Encyclopedia of Textiles*, American Fabrics Magazine, ed., Englewood Cliffs, N.J.: Prentice-Hall, Inc., 1960, p. 475.
‡ CIBA Chemical and Dye Company (Div. of CIBA Corporation).

The following dyeing processes are used on woven fabric:[2]

Process	Description	Fabric	Finished Product
Piece dyeing	Lengths of "gray" goods are immersed in dye enough times to obtain required brightness. Economical for small quantities	Woven	True in color
Union dyeing	A one-bath process in which the same color is made to penetrate different yarns or fibers	Combinations of yarns, such as wool worsted and orlon	Different yarns or fibers are the same color
Cross dyeing	A form of union dyeing which permits the dyeing of more than one color in a fabric woven of different fibers: one fiber resists the penetration of certain colors while others absorb them	Dacron, rayon, acrylic in combination with (for example) wool	Multicolored

Textile Printing   Man has applied colored designs to the surface of fabrics since earliest times, and printed fabrics are still widely used today. Below is a brief description of textile-printing methods:[3]

Process	Description	Area of Use
Resist printing	Areas not to be colored are covered with substance which resists dye. After dyeing, resist is removed; undyed portion is left as is or is colored by direct printing	Ancient Egypt as early as 600 B.C. India Java Peru Indonesia
Wood block printing	Design is carved in reverse on surface of wood blocks, then printed by applying colored dye to each block and pressing each block to surface of fabric in correct sequence	China, eighth century Egypt, fifth century Italy, twelfth century Germany (Rhine area) thirteenth and fourteenth centuries
Roller printing	Design is printed with engraved metal rollers, one color per roller. This method was at first limited to one color, but today many colors can be applied with great speed	England and France, 1780 to present
Screen printing	One screen, of silk, nylon, or metal thread, is used for each color in a design. Portion of pattern to be colored is cut out of masking film placed on screen. Color is applied to fabric by brushing or squeezing it through cutout portion of film. Successive screens are used for each color. Formerly a hand operation, this method is now mechanized for rapid, accurate production	France, mid-nineteenth century to present

Printing methods today vary according to location. The older methods are still used where labor is plentiful. But most textile printing is now done by the roller machine, whose great speed makes the finished article relatively inexpensive. The decorative-fabric trade still has a number of small printing establishments where hand-

[2] *Encyclopedia of Textiles*, American Fabrics Magazine, ed., Englewood Cliffs, N.J.: Prentice-Hall, Inc., 1960, p. 477.
[3] *Ibid.*, pp. 479–499.

printed fabrics are produced. The range in size of pattern, color, and shading is far greater in hand-printed fabrics than in roller-printed materials, but the cost is also higher.

Leather

Leather is often used for upholstery, and its beauty, like that of all natural materials, is in the variation of its color and texture. Unlike many other natural materials, however, leather must be put through a long and laborious process before it is ready for use: curing, trimming, washing, fleshing, bating, tanning, rolling, slicing, soaking, drying, finishing, softening, and finally dyeing. The architect or interior designer must be aware of the fact that the best hides are selected hides which have been gently sanded, or "snuffed," to remove marks or imperfections such as wire scratches and hair marks that were made during the life of the animal. These hides are termed *top-grain leathers*. For medium-priced furniture, leathers which are cut out of the hide just below the top grain are used. They are known as *deep buff leathers*.

The dyeing of leather is a high art. The colors are kept quite constant by spraying the leathers with dyes made to exact formulas. The number of colors that are available for upholstery will depend upon the manufacturer; some lines offer as many as 100. One representative line offers these thirty-one colors:

White	Larkspur blue
Bottle green	Turquoise
Medium yellow green	Light blue
Medium blue green	Tobacco brown
Olive green	Tan
Celadon green	Light rust
Deep fuchsia	Tangerine
Pinkish red	Golden yellow
Pink	Pale yellow
French ultramarine blue	Bittersweet
Cornflower blue	Deep greenish gold
Cerulean blue	Warm rust
Sand	Tan brown
Charcoal gray	Sable brown
Deep red	Lemon yellow
Black	

Before placing an order for a piece of furniture which is to be covered with leather, the architect or interior designer should ask for a color-selection card so that he will know whether the leather color he requires is available, or whether he needs a custom color. A rich tangerine, for instance, may not be available in a limited selection. The larger selections, of course, will include a number of shades of each color, and the larger the selection the greater the possibility that subtlety can be obtained. Some manufacturers provide custom colors at additional expense.

In addition to monotone colors and finishes, a number of top-grain leathers are available in two-tone effects which are given a patina. An examination of a rather extensive line will show that these are available in deep reds, gray green, tan, black, gunmetal, yellow green, tortoiseshell, and deep green. In still another group, a whitish glaze is given to yellow, pink, tan, gray, green, blue, and turquoise to produce a more pastel shade.

Leather may also be used for the tops of tables and desks or chests, as well as on doors. Pigskin has been used for flooring and wall covering. Leather in 6- by 6-inch or 12- by 12-inch tiles, mounted on a warp-free board, is available for use on walls. The leather usually has a gold-tooled design which is most effective.

Vinyl

While the early vinyls used for upholstery attempted to imitate leather colors, the manufacturers have now developed a range of colors and finishes all their own. For the most part, no attempt is made to copy the natural imperfections of leather: vinyl is treated frankly and honestly as a new material with its own exciting possibilities and uses. One of the lines recently introduced contains sixty-four colors which run the gamut from grayed colors to those of great brilliance. The color names themselves are descriptive and easily remembered: hyacinth, loganberry, raspberry, red apple, mandarin orange, tiger lily, fern, bluebell, etc.

It must be kept in mind that material for upholstery must be of a heavier weight than that usually used for walls and, in addition, it is well to select a rubber or stretch fabric that will "breathe." Manufacturers usually specify the uses for which their product is suited, and these recommendations should be heeded.

In addition to plain vinyls, embossed, printed, and "woven" patterns are available in a variety of colors. There are reptile patterns; fabric patterns such as *matelassé*, linen, moire, and burlap; self-stripe (two different textures on a single-color material); rough textures, such as straw; and even a quilted pattern.

SCREENS AND ROOM DIVIDERS

Portable screens, many of which combine utility with beauty, have been used for centuries in the Orient and in Europe. Varying in shape, color, and design according to origin, they at once provide a sense of privacy and a means for artistic expression. Perhaps the best-known and most expensive is the Chinese coromandel, notable for its carved intaglio design. Most often it is black, but sometimes it is brown or dark red, with the intaglio treated with gold or silver metallics or with color. Genuine antique coromandel screens are rare, and most of those made prior to the eighteenth century are in museums. Reproductions are available. Often the coromandel will be in panels 18 inches wide, and up to 12 feet high (see Plate XV).

Screens are frequently covered in antique French or Chinese wallpapers or scenic papers and can, therefore, be adapted to their setting. Japanese screens are painted on silk grounds or other types of paper; the subject matter usually relates to the great art of Japan. Scenes include florals, trees (often bamboos), and sensitively rendered landscapes. They are usually in black wash or color.

The shoji screen of Japan is made up of a series of panels and a delicate frame of narrow wood members. The pattern, consisting of a series of rectangles, is usually horizontal but occasionally vertical. A typical rectangle in a shoji screen might measure 8 7/8 by 10 5/8 inches. If the screens are made by excellent Japanese craftsmen, and if dried, seasoned cedar is used, the frames around each panel will be as narrow as 3/4 by 1 1/8 inches, and the minor members which form the rectangles will be as small as 5/16 inch. Rice paper, which is translucent and is made in a number of different patterns, is applied in a sheet on the back of the shoji. Its translucence gives the shoji a light, airy appearance. In the United States, where rice paper is not as readily available and where permanence is sought, plastic material often takes the place of rice paper. It, too, is translucent, and imbedded in it and forming its pattern are long white threads, leaves of green, rust, or red, butterflies, or bamboo.

Japanese closet doors, behind which bedding is stored during the day, are frequently treated with distinctive wallpapers that provide restrained color and pattern. Usually the major pattern in these papers is limited to the lower portion of the closet doors, and may consist of horizontal bands of chinese red, off-white, chartreuse, blue gray, and gold. More elaborate traditional papers include landscapes, seascapes, or leaf patterns; modern designs may include wide bands of fish swimming in a narrow band of sea. One of the most charming patterns that the author has seen consisted of a series of horizontal bands, beginning wide at the bottom and becoming steadily narrower as they approached the top. The bands were a soft shade of brown on a pale brown ground. Where color and objects are part of the pattern, they are usually tied together with a softly colored background—for instance, leaves of black and silver and white are placed on a background of golden yellow. Bronze and black fish swim in a blue-green sea. A range of mountains in a band at the bottom of a pair of closet doors will often be painted in several grayed shades, the nearer mountains dark blue green, the range immediately beyond white and gray, the most distant range pale purple.

A number of portable screens of a less restrained nature are available commercially. Most of them are made in panels of varying widths, each section being hinged to the next. Usually the frames are of wood; plastic, metal grilles, woven or carved wood, cane, fabric, or glass completes the panels. The faces may be flush or sunken.

Where wood is used, it may be natural finish or stained or it may be painted in any desired color. Other screens, or room dividers, are available in molded gypsum, leaded fiber glass, beaded glass, concrete filigree, and aluminum and other metals.

Decorative beads of wood, cork, glass, or plastic can also be effectively used as room dividers. Larger beads are suitable for large areas; smaller beads can be used in smaller spaces. Plastic beads can be supplied in such transparent colors as crystal, amber, aqua, green, sapphire, rose, red, and black. Wood beads are available in standard wood tones, pastel colors, or metallic colors. Wood beads and spindles are available in natural, tan, brown, black, and white enamel. Strings of beads can be hung from curtain rods, slit rods, fabric-covered dowels, screw eyes, or moldings.

Boris Kroll Fabrics, New York (Jacquard Linen Collection)

XIII.   Contemporary Fabric Collection

Window Shade Manufacturers Association, New York. Designed by Jack Lenor Larsen.

XIV. Living Room with Different Types of Window Shades for Variation

chapter seven

THE
APPLICATION OF
COLOR: FURNISHINGS

WINDOW TREATMENTS

Curtains

CURTAINS were originally used on cold walls and open doorways to keep heat in. Although windows were draped in the Orient as early as the sixth century, windows in the West were not curtained until mid-Renaissance times. Early curtain textiles were brilliant in color and included velvets and brocades from the East or from the workshops of Florence. The fabrics of the Louis XIV era were for the most part florals inspired by the Gardens of Versailles. In England during the reign of Queen Anne, patterns were larger than in France, and the curtains were used with wooden-based valances which were covered by matching fabric. In addition, cotton prints from India, and chintz, were used.

Fabric patterns have varied with architectural style. During the Rococo age, designs became irregular and curved, and the curtains themselves were in most cases unbalanced and unrestrained. During the era of Louis XIV, patterns were small, curved, and lacking in continuity. Subject matter included landscapes, flowers, plumes and feathers, and graceful female figures. During the time of Thomas Chippendale, the patterns of France included Chinese designs which were modified by French weavers. During this time also, cornices of gilt and japanned wood in an oriental style began to be used. Elaborate curves were employed to modify bare walls, and great amounts of gold cloth, as well as fringes of gold and silver, appeared in most drapery material used in Tudor houses. France was the center of drapery fashion for the almost 200-odd years that ended with Napoleon's reign. It is interesting to note that for a while after 1660, curtains grew fuller and more luxurious-looking and reflected the king's great wealth. During this period it was usual for a single glass curtain to cover an entire window, but toward the end of the seventeenth century curtains were designed in two panels with draw cords to open and close them.

During this period, pastel colors were used in France. Typical of these was Du Barry's Blushing Rose Pink. During the time immediately before the French Revolution, ostentation in interior design was tempered by the use of less ornate designs. Bouffant draperies began to disappear; proportions and details became balanced and more restrained in tone; patterns became smaller and less flowing. The classic trend, which began after the first Louis, continued. Draperies were relatively simple, with swags draped over a metal pole, sometimes pulled through large brass rings, and ending in a cascade or flat jabot.

The colors of the Directoire period were brilliant. They included bright red, green, deep yellow, black, and white. Patterns were formal and included narrow contrasting stripes. During the period of Napoleon, curtains were designed to appear to be carelessly hung, but in reality it was a studied carelessness: the fabric was carefully cut to lie in beautiful fashion over ornate poles that were made to look like spears, and eagles were often placed so as to catch the fabric in their beaks.

Calico was used in informal rooms during the Empire, but in formal rooms heavy fabrics, including satins, silks, moires, and embroidered velvets, were used. Occasionally there were three sets of draperies in contrasting colors such as gold, red, and green, or orange, pink, and blue. The colors were unusually harsh at that time. By the time Napoleon fell from power, the interior designs inspired by him also fell from grace. The French designers, having worked so long at developing those motifs, suddenly found themselves out of work. So it was that England became the center of style.

During the Victorian period, draperies were similar to those of the Empire in France, but they were heavier and larger. Their main function was to keep out light. Fabrics were heavy; they included velvets and damasks, most often in gold or dark red. With the advent of cheap machine-made fabric, lace was used at all windows—even those of the poor, who had curtains for the first time. Interior window shades, which had been used up until this time, continued to be used in England and in the United States.

In the eclectic period between Victorian and Modern, draperies were made in just about every style and material. During the mid-1920s, however, the idea of draping an entire window wall became popular. With this new design, the curtains could be opened during the daytime and closed during the dark hours to give the impression of a draped wall. The architect of that period of modern construction, reaching out for new forms and new methods, had no more use for historic designs in his fabrics than he had for historic forms in his architecture. He designed to eliminate reminders of the past, such as heavy Victorian curtains, and he threw his house open to sunlight. Where curtains were used, they were for the purpose of privacy only. Color, pattern, and form, devices previously used in draperies, were now incorporated into the architecture itself. The architectural space became a three-dimensional colored experience. Architecture no longer depended for its success upon things applied to it, but was in itself a complete, fresh, emotional experience. Suddenly architecture related to all mankind: not only to rulers, potentates, and presidents. Suddenly also, the designer of a contemporary house, instead of having to adhere to standard treatments, can individualize the curtain treatment of his building. If the window walls in his design need to be treated for privacy only, a plain fabric related in color to other elements in the room is used. If the windows are located high in the wall privacy is not a problem; no curtains are required, so they are omitted. If, on the other hand, an architectural space has been designed so that the curtains are expected to contribute to color and pattern, outer curtains are sometimes used with patterns reminiscent of famous contemporary paintings. Draperies for sun control may similarly be patterned—for example, with geometrics in oranges, brilliant greens, and blues, printed on light backgrounds. Or solid contemporary colors may be used.

The colors may be planned according to the scheme that the architect has in mind and may include such soft shades as gray beige, pale blue, white, or deep brilliant blues mixed with white or white and black. Sometimes curtain colors consist of alternate panels of, say, green, blue, and red. Often, of course, sheer glass curtains are used over a large glass area, while panels are used on either end of an opening.

If he wishes, the architect can substitute for draperies any number of other items—shades, bamboo blinds, vertical venetian blinds, woven aluminum blinds, etc. The contemporary architect has given himself a magnificent new freedom: he can do anything he wishes. He is no longer responsible to style makers; he makes his own style. In truth, the contemporary architect, in his continuing quest for new forms and colors, is more responsive to human needs and wishes than architects were in almost any other period of history

Shades and Blinds

There are, in addition to curtains, a number of other decorative means by which light may be controlled. These include venetian blinds of all kinds, woven blinds, matchstick blinds, roman shades, and window shades.

The standard-sized 2-inch-slat venetian blind and the newer narrow-slat blind are manufactured in silver, gray, medium blue, pastel blue, medium yellow green, pale green, pastel green, deep yellow, chartreuse, taupe, chinese red, pink, peach, ivory, gray beige, off-white, and oyster white. In addition, some blinds are made to imitate wood, and others linen. Tapes and cords for these blinds are available in colors to match or blend with the slats.

Woven Aluminum Blinds   Aluminum slats, about 5/16 inch wide, are woven into shades, blinds, or curtains. The slats are woven together by such items as chenille with metallic thread, plain cotton thread, or nylon webbing. These threads either match or contrast with the color of the blinds. For instance, a white blind might be woven with white chenille combined with a gold metallic yarn. This same warp can be used on pink, lilac, and pale green slats. Colorless nylon thread or white cotton thread, are also used in the weaving of narrow-slat blinds, which are available in white, eggshell, light beige, pink, pumpkin, chinese red, sand, lemon yellow, medium blue green, and sky blue. They can be installed as roll-up window shades, roman shades, cafe curtains, or vertical drapes.

Woven Wood Blinds   Other woven blinds are made of wood slats which are painted or stained. They are available in a wide variety of stitching and colors. Some of those manufactured by Tropicraft of San Francisco are described below:

1. Inner-core bamboo reed, with warp of two-ply cotton twine repeated every 2 inches
2. Philippine mahogany, with warp of 100 percent Dacron, heavy rug yarn, or rayon twist combination approximately every 4 inches
3. Slats and dowels of 1/4-inch walnut, with warp of fine cotton twine repeated every 7/8 inch
4. Wood dowels, 1/16-inch size, with warp of cotton yarn woven in bands of varying widths
5. Alternate 1/4-inch painted Philippine mahogany slats and painted reeds with warp of cotton two-ply *bouclé* and cut mylar foil in a 4-inch repeat
6. Painted aluminum slats with warp in a 4 1/4-inch repeat of viscose rayon, four-ply braid, cotton chenille and mylar foil
7. All-reed design with two sizes of chenille woven to produce an allover textured effect
8. Philippine mahogany slats with warp of rug yarn, cut-cotton chenille, viscose rayon *bouclé*, metallic *soutache*, and Lurex braid in a 10 1/2-inch repeat

Typical color combinations include wood slats in a soft gray with silver and silver-gray chenille; bands of white and gray chenille with accents of silver Lurex thread in a band about 7 inches wide; brown-stained slats with a 3-inch-wide band of off-white chenille, off-white rayon, beige *bouclé*, and a black accent. Matchstick blinds, natural or spray-painted, from 1/16 to 5/8 inch wide and woven with twine, are also extremely versatile.

Plastic Blinds Vertical folding blinds of translucent plastic (Jaylis) may be obtained in off-white, ivory, pale yellow, pastel green, red, sky blue, blue gray, butter yellow, peach, pink, brown, orange, black, turquoise, and marbleized colors such as green, white, blue, ivory, and pink. Accent strips are available.

Window Shades The contemporary window shade remains one of the most widely used and inexpensive methods of controlling light. The most popular roller shade is available in standard colors such as white, gray, and ivory in translucent and opaque styles of oil-painted cloth, glass fiber, or plastic film. Custom colors can be obtained also. Patterns in shade cloth impregnated with vinyl are available in such colors and patterns as:

1. Candy stripe—blue, pink, yellow, or green vertical stripes on white
2. Textured fabric with vertical gold thread in white, natural, pink, aqua, yellow, or green
3. Embroidered fine cotton lawn with silklike embroidery

A designer who wishes to coordinate the shades with other fabrics in the room, or with the wallpaper, may have the fabric or wallpaper laminated to an opaque or translucent shade cloth. In Plate XIV, for instance, the designer uses a handsome laminated window shade made from a baroque-stripe fabric in tangerine and white as the touchstone of the room scheme. When these shades are in the position shown, bottom-up shades on either side of the fireplace are pulled up to introduce large areas of the same bold color at that end of the room. This simple gambit provides a flexible use of color and pattern with very little effort, and forms the basis for a

FIG. 7.1 Sitting room

complete color scheme which includes beige ottomans, sofa cushions of nasturtium, deep orange, and gold, and an area rug in varying intensities of the tawny-color family.

Figure 7.1 shows the use of a crisp black and white fabric for walls as well as for laminated shades. To complete the color scheme, the designer uses brilliant white for window frames, wall dado, and the painted chairs. The white brick-patterned vinyl floor provides the background for the vivid bitter-green area rug and golden-yellow chair seats.

Figure 7.2, which illustrates a bedroom for a young girl, shows a sparse use of pattern on the shades to echo the fabric used for the bedspread, the canopy, and the chair cushions. The white shades are surrounded by a well-proportioned frame of brilliant tangerine. The tangerine of the frame, the french ultramarine blue of the bedposts, and the parrot-green floor all derive their colors from the pattern of the print. The walls are softly tinted with pink.

In Plate XV a combination of pull-up and bottom-up shades in Pompeian brown with black braid trim not only affords complete privacy, but also acts as a beautiful background for furniture and floor. Note that these colors were selected from those in the magnificent coromandel screen.

Figure 7.3, a country living room, illustrates the use of vertical-striped shades, which complement the horizontality of the room itself. The shades repeat the bright red color of the lacquer table and at the same time blend with the warm wood tone of paneling and furniture. The blue-bordered Chinese rug atop the polished floor adds a touch of richness, not only of color, but of texture.

It must be remembered that whatever the means used to control light, they will, if properly designed, minimize fading of carpets, wall coverings, furniture, wood, etc. Similarly, it must be kept in mind that the patterns of blinds which face the sun will also fade, and openwork blinds, if the sun problem is severe, may cause spot fading. These factors must be taken into consideration when light control is being planned.

Roman Shades Roman shades are among the most decorative means of controlling light. The suppliers of roman shades are very design-conscious and can furnish a number of stock patterns. A visit to a supplier's showroom will reveal designs that are decorative as wall hangings when they are in the closed position. For example, there is a Mondrian-like abstract pattern of colored rug-weaving wool that contains short horizontal stripes in the following colors on an off-white background: red-orange and brown; brown; chartreuse and orange; chartreuse and brown; red; brown, yellow, and orange; green and orange; orange; and orange, green, and red.

FIG. 7.2 Bedroom for a young girl

FIG. 7.4 *Hourglass pattern in roman shade*

FIG. 7.3 *Country living room*

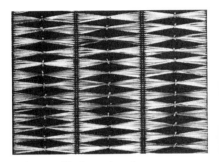

FIG. 7.5 *Horizontal pattern in roman shade*

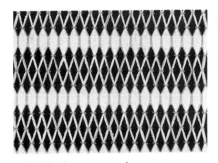

FIG. 7.6 *Lace pattern in roman shade*

Another pattern on a woven tan background contains hourglass figures which can be made in any combination of colors (Figure 7.4). In other patterns face yarns, in various colors, are woven on a solid wood back (Figures 7.5 and 7.6). Also available are a beige vertical woven pattern on 1/2-inch half dowels; a diagonal pattern, finished top and bottom with a horizontal pattern in french ultramarine blue; horizontal bands of bright yellow on a woven geometric background; vertical geometric patterns in curry with black edgings or chartreuse and white on a cocoa background. Custom designs can also be made, with or without backing, to the specifications of the designer. The open shades, as well as open-weave vertical blinds, are usually used where neither sun nor privacy is a problem.

Vertical Blinds Vertical blinds are particularly suited to large or tall openings, where vertical, rather than horizontal, control is desirable and where a uniform vertical tempo will complement the architecture as well as the interior. These consist of a series of vertical vanes mounted in carriers which are fastened at the top and bottom of the window opening. The vanes are approximately 3 inches wide and open to 90 degrees. The vanes may be obtained in a variety of materials, including opaque and flameproof Tontine in tan, gray blue, lemon yellow, light gray, eggshell, and white; celanese acetate in white, tan, gold, rose, warm gray and chartreuse; a number of plastic patterns in canvas, casement weave, shantung, grasscloth, etc. either translucent or opaque, and flameproof; and aluminum in a white mat finish. Special colors are obtainable for large jobs.

PAINTINGS

The paintings, pictures, or sculpture used in a room will depend upon the taste of the client, the style of the architectural space in which they are to be used, and, of course, the suitability of color, pattern, and subject. Good art can be used in residences, offices, and public buildings. Whether they are originals or copies does not matter if they are properly selected and placed. Often, the colors in a fine painting are the inspiration for the entire color scheme of a room or a series of architectural spaces.

The colors and intensities of a painting dictate the distance from which it should properly be viewed; this consideration should be borne in mind when choosing and hanging it. Dimensions will depend upon many factors, such as the size and proportion of the available space. If the painting is large, its hues and intensities must be considered so that it is part of the room and not an isolated note. Fitness of subject matter should also be considered: one executive the author knows was chagrined to find that a seminude which he had hung in a conference room caused more discussion than the problems on the agenda. A large seascape with realistic waves in a doctor's reception room can cause some patients to become nauseated. Prints to be used in the psychiatric unit of a hospital should consist of peaceful landscapes in quiet colors; violent "motion" in a painting will sometimes cause violent reactions in a mentally ill person.

While some of the above considerations need not be regarded in residential work, other factors, such as architectural style, must be taken into account. An English period room will usually benefit by the use of narrative and disciplined art. Up to about the last quarter of the eighteenth century, a good English interior included only portraits since other forms of painting were monopolized by the Italian and Flemish masters. The grand style of English portrait painting treated color with subtlety and restraint. For example, Sir Joshua Reynolds's (1723–1792) *Lady Elizabeth Delme and Her Children* (Mellon Collection, National Gallery of Art) contains soft shades of pink, blue and white, with gray-brown trees and a low-key background which conveys dignity and good taste. Thomas Gainsborough's (1727–1788) *Portrait of Mrs. Richard Brinsley Sheridan* illustrates the same point. The lady's dress is a pastel pink; all colors around it, including those of the sky and trees, are soft gray green. In contrast, French portraits of this period frequently show the use of freer technique and bolder colors, such as the bright yellow and terra-cotta in Jean Honoré Fragonard's (1732–1806) *A Young Girl Reading.*

A nineteenth-century English room often included still life paintings in natural colors—for example, bright red berries contrasted with a blue dish and silver bowl, all offset by a landscape in a window, as in John F. Francis' (1808–1886) still life *Strawberries and Cream;* or the naturalistic colors, deep and rich, of Winslow Homer's seascapes. In addition to oil paintings, nineteenth-century English rooms often included engravings, Audubon prints, and Currier and Ives prints, with color varying according to subject.

If the periods preceding the contemporary period were for the most part characterized by realism, it may be said that the contemporary artist "expresses what he perceives; he perceives what he expresses."[1] In other words, if we remember that we see what we learn to see, that we see what we *want* to see, and that what we perceive is shaped by internal subjective factors as well as by external optical laws, then we can understand that the paintings which are used in architectural spaces can be successful without telling a story: they can be successful if they contain color and

[1] Herbert Read, *A Concise History of Modern Painting,* New York: Frederick A. Praeger, Inc., 1959, p. 12.

Window Shade Manufacturers Association, New York. Designed by Paul Krauss, A.I.D.

XV. Window Shades in Study

Du Pont Textile Fibers. James Merrick Smith, A.I.D., and Jini Costello, A.I.D., Designers.

XVI. Florida Living Room

pattern which sets the color tone for the area and contributes to it by its very size, shape, and placement.

In some modern art, objects are differentiated only by luminosity. If subject matter is disregarded, the quality of a painting can be judged by (among other things) how pleasing an abstract pattern it makes. In, for instance, Henri Matisse's *Still Life with Goldfish* (1911), the importance lies in the place occupied by the objects, empty spaces around them, i.e. proportion and composition.

Perhaps the most important difference between the art we term "modern" and that which preceded it is in the colors used. Colors suddenly become, as in Raoul Dufy's *The Artist and His Model in the Studio at Le Havre* (1929), brilliant light and dark blues, brilliant reds, orange, and pink. Compare this with the controlled impetuosity obtained by Paul Gauguin in his *The Moon and the Earth* (1893).

Otto Mueller in his *Gipsies with Sunflowers* (1927) used large areas of brilliant yellow and strong green. Louis Marcoussis, in *Two Poets* (1929), used a bright orange and green against a background of neutral colors.

But even within this period, there are differences in the way artists use color. Pieter Mondriaan in his *Composition with Red, Yellow and Blue* (1921) strategically placed relatively small amounts of blue, purple, orange, and yellow in a framework of black against a light background. Kazimir Malevich in his *Suprematist Composition* (1915) used red violet, blue violet, jade green, orange, and chinese red, as well as black and pink, in a disciplined and dynamic composition. Arshile Gorky, in *Agony* (1947), used bright shades of pink contrasted with spots of dark blue. Giuseppe Santomaso used brilliant deep yellow, oranges, and various shades of green on a bright yellow background in his composition entitled *Reds and Yellows of Harvest Time* (1957). Similarly, Ernst Wilhelm Nay in *Alpha* (1957) combines brilliant reds, blues, and greens in large patterns.

The colors used in many famous contemporary paintings have inspired contemporary interior color schemes. While pastel shades are often used today, they are usually employed as a foil for brilliant spots of color (see Plate XVIII). Many architects and designers of contemporary interiors, inspired by the colors of modern paintings, use relatively large amounts of brilliant color, such as deep green, red, brilliant yellow, yellow orange, spectrum blue, gold, pumpkin, or emerald green. With these brilliant colors, however, one finds carpets and furniture in supporting shades of gray black, putty, tan, brown, and deep gray green (see Plate XIV). For example, a putty sofa and red-orange chairs might be used in front of a pumpkin wall with a black and white painting on it; a putty sofa and emerald-green chair in front of a spectrum-blue wall with a black and white print on it; or a black sofa and orange chairs in front of a spectrum-red wall with a painting in red, green, brown, and white. Just as often, bright red, orange, blue, green, or brown will be used in front of a white wall where the paintings are bright. To achieve quiet elegance, one may use deep brown furniture, a pumpkin carpet, and curtains of pale pumpkin or white. In such a room, a small bowl of yellow flowers will provide a superb accent; drawings or paintings should be muted. With black and white drawings or paintings, such as Picasso's *Four Ballet Dancers*, black and white are often used in parts of the room. "Op art," or "perceptual abstraction," uses both brilliant color and complex arrangements of black and white. Regardless of subject matter or period, black and white can usually be used successfully with spots of brilliant color (see Plate XXIV).

The successful selection of colorful accessories is not an accident. One simply cannot select them at random if he hopes to complete and complement an otherwise-integrated color scheme. The range of accessories available is so wide and so personal that it is possible in the space available here merely to establish guidelines. A sense of fitness is important. Personal taste is perhaps the most usual criterion for the selection of accessories, but the style of the room should be considered.

Those who design period rooms, if they are purists, select accessories which were popular during the respective periods in which they seek inspiration. Those who prefer antique accessories hunt constantly for rare, appropriate pieces. For instance, if one is designing in the Colonial style, accessories might include tall case clocks, pewter, kitchenware, pictures and maps, firearms, and lanterns. If the objects are authentic, the colors will be correct. If one is doing a room in the style of the early eighteenth century one might include oriental china and English staffordshire, wedgwood, chelsea, and derby, as well as sandwich-glass items. On the other hand, if the room is eighteenth-century French, crystal chandeliers, wall brackets, mirrors, sèvres porcelain, and marble busts are appropriate. The designer who prefers to blend more than one style in a room has his choice of accessories from the styles that he combines. It is perfectly acceptable to use a small number of antique accessories in a contemporary room. A group of engravings or prints made centuries ago will usually add charm to a contemporary room if subject matter is appropriate, the size is correct, and the grouping and placing are attractive. (Fig. 7.7)

Thanks to the excellence of commercial exchange, rare accessories may now be obtained with relative ease. While the world traveler enjoys the thrill of discovering rare accessories, he soon finds that many are available in his own country, where he may select them at leisure for color and appropriateness. However, the truly rare items a traveler discovers abroad are the things he is likely to enjoy most. Imagine the anticipation with which the captains of New England clipper ships were greeted when they returned from the Orient with silk, tea chests, screens, and canton china!

As emphasized earlier, the colors of accessories must relate to the general color scheme of a room (see Plates XVI, XVIII, XXI, XXII, and XXIV). They should contribute to and be enhanced by it. A chinese-red oriental chest will contribute only if it harmonizes or complements the total color scheme, and if the chinese red is repeated elsewhere in the room. A green bowl with yellow chrysanthemums will look good in a white-and-yellow room with a pale green carpet. Objects of natural-finished wood will look good almost anywhere. Copper kitchen utensils and orange-brown natural-baked clay pots will look good in a kitchen-dining area where warm tones of orange and off-white are used on walls and floor. A curry-yellow porcelain bowl on a black base will key an entire room of yellow, green, and white if it is placed strategically. A brass filigreed jewel box will be quite at home in a room where the colors are predominantly warm; the same type of box made of silver or pewter will add a great deal to a room which is cool in color.

From the above it may be seen that the color of accessories must contribute to the room, and the room must contribute to the accessories.

The colors one uses will depend upon the job at hand: a bright and happy room calls for rich, deep accessories. A subdued room, in which all of the colors are, say, restful grays and browns, will be enhanced by bright accessories.

No interior is complete without plants, flowers, or both. If possible, the beauties of an exterior garden should be continued inside by means of large glass areas. If not, plants or flowers can be artfully placed in at least the most important rooms to accentuate their colors. Flowers may be placed in glass or pottery vases whose colors complement those of the flowers and the room. A vase of pale yellow roses will look good in a yellow-green room, pink roses in a pink and blue room, pale greenish-white dogwood in a yellow, green, and orange room, and red, purple, and white in a blue and white room. Yellow-hearted daisies will always look good in a black and white room. Green plants or vases of green leaves will harmonize with almost any color scheme.

The number of accessories should be limited, or clutter will result. As accessories are usually small and easily moved, seasonal changes may be made. If a collection of items is to be displayed, a special cupboard or cabinet probably will enhance its effectiveness.

LAMPS

Although modern architectural lighting for the most part precludes the use of lamps, they can be used to advantage if their size, color, and shape are determined in the initial study of an architectural space. While those for reading differ in size and color from those used for general light, all lamps in an area should have certain similarities. For instance, the inside reflecting surface of lampshades should be white, and there should be no direct transmitted reflected glare. The lamps should contribute to the room's general illumination by providing a generous amount of upward light. The

FIG. 7.7   Contemporary living room

bulb in a lamp should be located as low as possible so as to spread light over a wide area, but should not, of course, be visible from a sitting position. Floor lamps should be located behind the user to protect his eyes from direct glare.

The materials for lamps will vary according to the period of the room in which they are to be used. Materials for lamps to be used in traditional rooms are most appropriate if they reflect the materials and are compatible with the artifacts of that period. An Early American room, for instance, may have lamps of brass, pewter, copper, wood, or pottery; those in a contemporary room might be made of any of these, or of stainless steel, chromed metal, ceramics, enamelware, plastic, marble, crystal, leather, iron, or wood. The wood may be used alone or in combination with other materials—for example, brass. A material, traditional or otherwise, is acceptable if it harmonizes with the colors of the room and if it is appropriate in form and size.

The lamp's base and shade colors, and its scale as well, must fit the total design. In many cases, when the bases of the lamps are of a material that can be painted, colors which complement or harmonize with the rest of the room are used.

The color of the shade and its trim must be selected to harmonize with the base, and the shade material itself must be appropriate in texture. An off-white with a yellowish overtone may be acceptable in a yellow room, while a bluish-white will be appropriate in a blue or green room. The material used for shades can be silk (taffeta or shantung), paper, grasscloth, or plastic. All of these are available in many colors. A lamp must be considered as a piece of sculpture, and its shape, form, and color must be treated as integral parts of the total three-dimensional composition in which it is to be used.

Courtesy of William Pahlmann, F.A.I.D.

XVII.   Entrance Foyer

Courtesy of William Pahlmann, F.A.I.D.

XVIII.   Living Room

Private Residence. Ezra Stoller (ESTO) Photographer.

XIX. Dining Room

XX.   Living Room

Residence by Eero Saarinen and Alexander Girard. Ezra Stoller (ESTO) Photographer.

XXI. Living Room

Designed by Judith and Richard Newman. Ezra Stoller (ESTO) Photographer.

XXII.   Storage-wall Arrangement in Converted Brownstone

Interior by Helmut Jacoby. Alexandre Georges, Photographer.

XXIII.   Town House

Du Pont Textile Fibers. Jerome Manashaw, A.I.D., and Edyth McCoon, A.I.D., Designers.

XXIV. Penthouse Apartment

U.S. Plywood Corp., New York. Frederick Davis, A.I.D., Designer.

XXV.   Art Collector's Study, Weldwood Walnut Panelling

U.S. Plywood Corp., New York. Tom Lee, A.I.D., Designer.

XXVI.   Hunting Lodge, Weldwood Brown Wormy Chestnut Panelling

Brunswick Executive Offices. Skidmore, Owings & Merrill, Architects. Ezra Stoller (ESTO), Photographer.

XXVII. Office Area

National Geographic Society. Edward Durrell Stone, Architect. Ezra Stoller (ESTO), Photographer.

XXVIII.   Executive Conference Area, National Geographic Society Building

John Deere Co. Eero Saarinen & Associates, Architects. Ezra Stoller (ESTO), Photographer.

XXIX.   Executive Office

Tennessee Gas. Skidmore, Owings & Merrill, Architects. Ezra Stoller (ESTO), Photographer.

XXX.   Executive Office, Ten-Ten Travis Building

XXXI. Hotel Restaurant

Courtesy of William Pahlmann, F.A.I.D.

XXXII.   Hotel Lobby

CONCLUSION

From the foregoing description of materials, furniture, and furnishings, one may see that the number of available colors is great indeed. At no other time in the history of the world have so many hues, tints, and shades been available to so many people. No longer is the choice of color limited to the chief of state, the church, or the wealthy. The rules for using color have multiplied. Color has truly become a universal property.

But the very freedom presented by this universality imposes responsibilities. One may use color as he wishes only if it does not adversely affect those around him. Color can be used as a reward or a penalty.

In any case, it is certain that this freedom will continue to increase. New hues are appearing every day; travelers will continue to carry colors and color combinations from one part of the world to another. Architectural style is changing almost daily, and the color requirements for new architectural forms are changing too. Manufacturers will continue to diversify; chemists and physicists will develop new products in new colors. Methods of lighting will change. Architects and interior designers will continue to absorb and synthesize the new colors, developing guidelines for their use as each new color appears in the color explosion of the future. Out of the raw materials provided by technicians, the architect and interior designer will continue to provide leadership in the development and use of color for architectural spaces which will be functional, appropriate, and elegant. All who are engaged in the design of interiors will agree that successful interior design is dependent upon long and careful training and a thorough knowledge of materials and their potentialities. While color in itself occupies an important position in the design of an interior, it cannot, of course, be used apart from texture, scale, proportion, and form. Rules for the use of color should be mastered. But in the end, the success of a color scheme will depend not only upon the color designer's ability to use any given color system, but also upon his natural ability, his taste, and a certain amount of inspiration and emotion.

ACKNOWLEDGMENTS

This book was, to a great extent, made possible by the cooperation of architects, interior designers, and those engaged in the manufacture and supply of those items which are used in the design of interior architectural spaces. To all those who gave freely of their time and information I offer my deep appreciation. I also appreciate the material loaned to me by many individual companies, societies, associations, etc. My sincere apologies are extended to those whose names I have have omitted in discussing individual materials which, because of lack of space, could not be included. I also wish to thank the many persons for photographs loaned to me, and to those whose photographs could not be included, also due to lack of space, I offer my apologies.

ALL-COLOR DESIGN & MARKETING, INC., New York, N.Y.
  Lorain Fawcett

AMERICAN BILT-RITE RUBBER CO., INC., Trenton, N.J.
  R. D. Schmid, Advertising Manager

AMERICAN CARPET INSTITUTE, New York, N.Y.
  E. N. Connett

AMERICAN OLEAN TILE CO., Lancaster, Pa.
  Louis D. Methfessel, Advertising Manager
  James G. Dox, New York, N.Y.

ARMSTRONG CORK CO., Lancaster, Pa.
  R. K. Marker, Public Affairs Dept.

BARWICK MILLS, E. T., INC., Chamblee, Ga.

BERGEN BLUESTONE CO., INC., Paramus, N.J.
  Mrs. G. O. Hansen
  Glenn Nilsen

BIGELOW-SANFORD, INC., New York, N.Y.
  Louise Sloane, Public Relations

BOWEN, LOUIS W., New York, N.Y.

BRENEMAN-HARTSHORN, INC., Cincinnati, Ohio

DIRECTIONAL FURNITURE, New York, N.Y.

DUPONT CO., New York, N.Y.
  Judith Mortenson, Public Relations

FIELDS, EDWARD, INC., New York, N.Y.
  Jack Fields

FINE HARDWOODS ASSOCIATION, Chicago, Ill. 60611
  E. Howard Gatewood, Executive Vice-president

FORMICA CORP., Cincinnati, Ohio
  David S. Perkins, Manager of Publicity

GENERAL ELECTRIC CO., Large Lamp Department,
  Nela Park, Cleveland, Ohio 44112
  Kaye Leighton, Residential Lighting Specialist
  George Matilo

GRACIE, CHARLES R. & SONS, INC., New York, N.Y.

GREEFF FABRICS, INC., New York, N.Y.
  Albert Leach

HARDWOOD PLYWOOD MANUFACTURERS ASSOCIATION,
  Arlington, Va. 22206
  William J. Groah, Laboratory Manager

HARRIS MANUFACTURING CO., Johnson City, Tenn. 37602
  Robert Harkins, Manager, Advertising Promotion & Sales

KATZENBACH & WARREN, INC., New York, N.Y.

KITTINGER COMPANY, INC., Buffalo, N.Y.
  Mason Reed, New York, N.Y.

KNOLL ASSOCIATES, INC., New York, N.Y.

KRAUSS, PAUL, INC., New York, N.Y.

KROLL, BORIS, FABRICS, New York, N.Y.

LEVOLOR-LORENTZEN, INC., Hoboken, N.J.

LOUVER-DRAPE, New York, N.Y., and Santa Monica, Calif.
  Paul Hopewood

MARBLE INSTITUTE OF AMERICA, INC., Washington, D.C. 20004
  Don Hagerich, Managing Director

MARSHALL, WILLIAM L., LTD., New York, N.Y. 10016
  Thomas A. Ryan, Jr., Vice-president

MARTIN SENOUR PAINTS, Chicago, Ill.
  Margaret Hutchinson, Color Stylist

THE NATIONAL TERRAZZO & MOSAIC ASSOCIATION, INC.,
Arlington, Va. 22209

PAHLMANN, WILLIAM, ASSOCIATES, INC., New York, N.Y.

PITTSBURGH PLATE GLASS CO., New York, N.Y.

PRATT & LAMBERT, INC., New York, N.Y.

PROBBER, HARVEY, SHOWROOMS, INC., New York, N.Y.
10022
  Harvey Probber

RISOM JENS DESIGN, INC., New York, N.Y.

SCALAMANDRE WALLPAPER, INC., New York, N.Y.

STARK CARPET CORPORATION, New York, N.Y.
  Jack Soskin

TILE COUNCIL OF AMERICA RESEARCH CENTER, Princeton, N.J.
  Dr. J. V. Fitzgerald, Director

TROPICRAFT, SAN FRANCISCO, San Francisco, Calif.

UNITED STATES PLYWOOD CORPORATION, New York, N.Y. 10017
  Martha Nold, Public Relations

VICRTEX SALES CORPORATION, New York, N.Y. 10022
  K. W. Hanlon, Vice-president

WALBEAD, INC., New York, N.Y.

WHITTIER-RUHLE MILLWORK CO., Ridgefield, N.J.

WINDOW MODES, INC., New York, N.Y. 10022
  Sidney Siegel

WINDOW SHADE MANUFACTURERS ASSOCIATION, New York, N.Y. 10017
  Hilda D. Sachs

CREDITS
for Black and White Illustrations

BIBLIOGRAPHY

AIA Honor Award 1949–1961, *Mid Century Architecture in America,* edited and with an Introduction by Wolf von Eckart, Foreword by Philip Will, Jr., FAIA, Baltimore: The Johns Hopkins Press, 1961.

Albers, Josef, *Interaction of Color,* New Haven, Conn.: Yale University Press, 1963.

American Carpet Institute, Inc., *Four Sales Manuals,* New York.

American Olean Tile Company, *Tile Manufacture.*

Arms, Brock, AIA, AID, NSID, "*Interiors: What Is the Architects' Role,*" The Octagon, Washington, D.C.: AIA Journal, Official Magazine of the AIA, December, 1966.

Baker, Hollis, *Furniture in the Ancient World,* A Giniger Book in Association with The Macmillan Company, New York: 1966.

Birren, Faber, *Color in Interiors: Historical and Modern,* New York: Whitney Library of Design, 1963.

———, *New Horizons in Color,* New York: Reinhold Publishing Corporation, 1955.

Boger, H. Batterson, *The Traditional Art of Japan,* Garden City, N.Y.: Doubleday & Company, Inc., 1964.

Building Research Institute, *Identification of Color for Buildings,* New York: Building Research Institute, 1962.

Burnham, R. W., R. M. Hanes, C. J. Bartelson, *Color: A Guide to Basic Facts and Concepts,* New York: John Wiley & Sons, Inc., 1963.

Burris, Meyer E., *Color Design in the Decorative Arts,* Englewood Cliffs, N.J.: Prentice-Hall, Inc., 1945.

———, *Contemporary Color Guide,* New York: William Helburn, Inc., 1947.

Ciba Review 1962/1–6: Published by Ciba Ltd., Basel, Switzerland. Represented in the United States by Ciba Chemical and Dye Company (Division of Ciba Corp.), Fair Lawn, N.J. p. 30, Vol. 4.

Ciba Review, Vol. Nos. 1–24, Sept. 1937 to Aug. 1939.

Ciba Review, Vol. 1, 1963, pp. 11–22.

Commery, E. W., and C. Eugene Stephenson, *How to Decorate and Light Your Home,* New York: Coward-McCann, Inc., 1955.

Cooke, H. L. (Curator), *British Painting in the National Gallery of Art,* Washington, D.C.: Publications Fund, National Gallery of Art, 1960.

———, *French Painting of the Sixteenth and Eighteenth Centuries in the National Gallery of Art,* Washington, D.C.: Publications Fund, National Gallery of Art, 1959.

Dantyagi, Susheela, *Fundamentals of Textiles and Their Care,* Bombay: Orient Longmans, Ltd., 1964.

Denny, Grace Goldena, *Fabrics and How to Know Them,* Philadelphia: J. B. Lippincott Company, 1923.

The Development of Various Decorative and Upholstery Fabrics, New York: F. Schumacher & Co., 1924.

Encyclopedia of Textiles, American Fabrics Magazine (ed.), Englewood Cliffs, N.J.: Prentice-Hall, Inc., 1960, 702 pp.

Evans, Ralph M., *An Introduction to Color,* New York: John Wiley & Sons, Inc., 1948.

Fletcher, Sir Bannister, *A History of Architecture on the Comparative Method,* New York: Charles Scribner's Sons, 1928

Focillan, Henri, *The Art of the West in the Middle Ages, Vol. I, Romanesque Art,* London: Phaidon Press, Ltd., 1963.

Gardner, Helen, *Art through the Ages,* New York: Harcourt Brace & World, Inc., 1936.

Glazier, Richard, *Historic Textile Fabrics,* New York: Charles Scribner's Sons, 1923.

Graves, Maitland, *Color Fundamentals,* New York: McGraw-Hill Book Company, 1952.

Hardwood Plywood Manufacturers Association, *Versatile Hardwood Plywood,* Arlington, Va.: 1966.

House & Garden, *The Modern Interior,* Robert Harling (ed.), Vogue House, Hanover Square, London W-1: The Condé Nast Publications, Ltd., 1964.

Huntington, W. C., *Building Construction,* 3d ed., New York: John Wiley & Sons, Inc., 1963.

Illuminating Engineering Society, *IES Lighting Handbook,* 3d ed., I.E.S., 345 East 47 St., New York City: 1959.

Inter-society Color Council, *Inter Chem: The Story of Color and Demonstration in Color Perception,* 50-page booklet, Interchemical Corp., 1965.

Jacobson, Egbert, *Basic Color: An Interpretation of the Ostwald Color System,* Chicago: Paul Theobald & Company, 1948.

Ketchum, Howard, *Color Planning for Business and Industry,* Harper & Row, Publishers, Incorporated, 273 pp., color illus. 8 pages, 1958.

Koblo, Martin, *World of Color,* New York: McGraw-Hill Book Company, 1962.

Koch, Robert, *Louis Tiffany, Rebel in Glass,* New York: Crown Publishers, Inc., 1964.

Lowry, Bates, *The Visual Experience: An Introduction to Art,* New York: Harry N. Abrams, Inc. and Englewood Cliffs, N.J.: Prentice-Hall, Inc., 1964.

Lynes, Russell, *The Tastemakers,* New York: Harper & Row, Publishers, Incorporated, 1949, 1953, 1954.

Morse, Edward S., *Japanese Homes and Their Surroundings,* New York: Dover Publications, Inc., 1961 (Orig. 1886).

Munsell, A. H., *A Color Notation:* A measured color system, based on the three qualities, hue, value and chroma, with illustrative models, charts, and a course of study arranged for teachers, 2d ed., Boston: George H. Ellis Co., 1907.

Parker, Harry, C. M. Gay, J. W. MacGuire, *Materials and Methods of Architectural Construction,* 3d ed., New York: John Wiley & Sons, Inc., 1958.

Read, Herbert, *A Concise History of Modern Painting,* New York: Frederick A. Praeger, Inc., 1959.

Rorimer, James J., *The Cloisters,* New York: The Metropolitan Museum of Art, 1939.

Schlumberger, Eveline, "The Case of the Ambierle Altarpiece" *Realites,* July, 1965.

Seitz, William C., *The Responsive Eye,* New York: The Museum of Modern Art, 1965.

Sellars, R. W., *The Essentials of Logic,* Boston: Houghton Mifflin Company, 1925.

Smith, Bradley, *Japan: A History in Art,* New York: Simon & Schuster, Inc., 1964.

Stenico, Arturo, *Roman and Etruscan Painting,* New York: The Viking Press, Inc., 1963.

Terry, Charles S., *Masterworks of Japanese Art,* Rutland, Vt., and Tokyo, Japan: Charles E. Tuttle Co., 1956.

Tokyo National Museum, *100 Masterpieces from the Collection,* Tokyo: 1959.

U.S. Department of Commerce, *Ceramic Tile for Floors and Walls,* Simplified Practice Recommendation, R61-61, Washington, D.C., Government Printing Office, 1961.

Whitney, F. L., *The Elements of Research,* Englewood Cliffs, N.J.: Prentice-Hall, Inc., 1942.

Woldering, Irmgard, *The Art of Egypt—The Time of the Pharoahs,* Anne E. Keep (trans.), New York: Crown Publishers, Inc., 1963.

Wright, F. L., *The Natural House,* New York: Horizon Press, 1954.

Whiton, Sherrill, *Elements of Interior Decoration,* Philadelphia: J. B. Lippincott Company, 1944.

INDEX

Knoche, L., 30